A
SIMPLE
PATH

MOTHER TERESA

A SIMPLE PATH

Compiled by
Lucinda Vardey

Ballantine Books
New York

ISBN: 0-345-40571-4

Manufactured in the United States of America
First Ballantine Books International Trade Paperback Edition:
December 1995
10 9 8 7 6 5 4 3 2 1

CONTENTS

꙰

HOW
THIS
BOOK
CAME
ABOUT

❧

"*I can tell you about my path,*" said Mother Teresa, "*but I'm only a little wire—God is the power. Talk to the others, the sisters and the brothers and the people who work with them. Some are not Christians, talk to them. You will know what it is when you see it. It is very beautiful.*"

This book, *A Simple Path*, began several years ago when Omer Ahmed, a film producer colleague, arranged a meeting with Mother Teresa to discuss ideas for a book and film project. Although he has lived in London for forty-five years, Omer comes originally from India and his great-grandparents used to own land in the Tiljala and Motijheel districts of Calcutta. Tiljala is, today, on the other side of the railway track from Mother Teresa's home for the mentally handicapped, and Motijheel is the area in which she started her first home. Omer's family are Muslim but all of his sisters were educated at Loreto, where Mother Teresa taught in the thirties and forties. His family has long supported the work of the Missionaries of Charity.

We had become interested in exploring the extraordinary potency of Mother Teresa as a symbol of love in action. Her impact on the public imagination has been compared to the ripples a stone makes when it is thrown into a calm pool of water. For many non-Christians, Mother Teresa represents a form of Christianity they can wholeheartedly respect.

Yet although most of Mother Teresa's biographical details are now well known, what is not widely understood is why she and the women and men of her order live in the way they do—and whether, in this age of complication and confusion, she has anything relevant and accessible to say to those searching for a better way of life at the end of the twentieth century. By listening to what she said, seeing what she did, and why, could we learn more about how to really connect with the people around us? Could Mother Teresa and the Missionaries of Charity offer hope in what seemed like a difficult world?

It was with these, and many other, questions in mind that we came to be waiting at the Mother House of the Missionaries of Charity in Calcutta, one hot July day in 1994. As in all the houses of the Order around the world, the atmosphere was functional and very busy. Visitors were being dealt with politely but were not allowed to distract from the important work of helping the poorest of the poor.

At first, Mother Teresa was unsure at the prospect of yet another book. She said she doubted if any more words would bring anyone closer to understanding the meaning of her mission. It was all so simple, she said. Why should anyone need a guide to her simple path? All we, or anyone else, needed to do was to pray, and start loving one another more. First, we should become as familiar as possible with the work of the Missionaries of Charity by visiting Shishu Bhavan (the children's home); Prem Nivas (the center for leprosy patients in Titagarh, run by the Missionaries of Charity brothers); Nirmal Hriday (the home for the dying and destitute); and Prem Dan (the home for TB sufferers and mentally handicapped patients).

We visited these, and other homes, several times, and the experience made us absolutely sure that a book which would help us learn how to pray, how to love more easily, how best to offer service to others, and so on was indeed needed. These questions could perhaps be dealt with readily by the Missionaries of Charity, but those of us in the West needed a series of clear and coherent steps to help us follow the path.

At this point the religious writer Lucinda Vardey was chosen to compile the book and joined us in further research. During the following months, we were offered more and more support with the project by Mother Teresa and her community and began by talking to Mother Teresa at great length on a wide range of subjects. We then discussed her approach and the work of the Missionaries of Charity with specific sisters and brothers in India and in the West, whom Mother introduced. Next, our search led us to individuals from many parts of the world who had volunteered in the Missionaries of Charity homes—and we asked them to share their experiences and feelings about their work, too. Finally, Mother Teresa and her Order saw and approved the text and wished it well. The results are laid out in the succeeding pages.

JOHN CAIRNS, 1995

INTRODUCTION

Whatever our views of Mother Teresa as a courageous missionary or a living saint, she has made a lasting impression. We all have an opinion about her. She has been recognized as an exponent of world peace and often appears on lists of the world's ten most admired women. Yet she herself has never claimed to be, or to be doing, anything extraordinary.

But how much do we actually know of Mother Teresa's philosophy and her work? When we take the trouble to look beyond the public view, we find that her faith and her clarity of purpose give us powerful lessons in the ways of loving, serving, and respecting our fellow human beings, especially those who are poor and deprived. She practices what she preaches. She treads a simple path, and it can be followed by anyone.

In the past, we have had extraordinary spiritual leaders sent to us at times when the world urgently needed leadership and spiritual guidance. These people, of vast spiritual strength, were clearly linked to the divine and in many cases were revolutionary in their teachings. One such figure was the charismatic St. Francis of Assisi.

Born in twelfth-century Italy, Francis sold all his possessions to obey Christ's call to repair His Church. Initially, Francis devoted his life to living in poverty (wearing only a coarse robe and begging for food) and to caring for lepers and outcasts. Later, he founded an order of friars and was influential in reforming the then very rich, and frequently misguided, Catholic Church. By the time of his death, he had gathered more than five thousand professed monks, priests, and nuns to carry on his work. Today, the Franciscan order thrives as one of the largest religious orders in the world.

St. Francis was a radical in his day—was even perceived as a heretic—because he offered a fresh view of the Christian life by living as a beggar, believing in providence, and closely following the teaching of the Gospel. But what was also unusual about him was that he reformed his own religion from within the institutional Church rather than by breaking away from it. Mother Teresa's life has many similarities to that of Francis. Her path is also through poverty, simplicity, and adherence to the teachings of Christ, and because of this she has been viewed as a progressive in the present fundamentalist framework of the patriarchal Church. Yet she preaches her love and peace in action in a world still lacking in strong female leaders and from one of the largest and poorest and most polluted cities in Asia.

Mother Teresa received God's call to serve the poorest of the poor in 1946 and began, in a small way, by caring for one sick and dying person whom she found on the streets of Calcutta. Today, she is head of the Missionaries of Charity, a religious order that she formed with the Vatican's blessing in 1950. Over the last forty-five years, when vocations have been slowly declining in the Catholic Church, the numbers of the Missionaries of Charity sisters and brothers have been growing and now total more than four thousand worldwide.

Sisters and brothers of the Missionaries of Charity practice their life of poverty with the absolute faith that this will bring them nearer to God. They trust and believe in His providence and, like Francis, live and work only through the generosity of others. Also, like Francis, they live what they teach—including not owning any more than the poor they serve. They eat frugally and possess only two sets of clothes, a pair of sandals, a bucket, a metal plate, the basic utensils, and sparse bedding. Their community life is built upon the words of the Gospel—the Christian way of prayer, love, forgiveness, nonjudgment, humility, truth, and total surrender to the Word.

A brief look at some of the landmarks in Mother

Teresa's life helps to shed light on the many facets of her character and on the aim of her work. Mother Teresa was born Agnes Gonxha Bojaxhiu in Skopje, Albania, on August 26, 1910, the youngest of three children. She had a comfortable childhood—her father was a building contractor and importer; her mother was strict but loving, with a deep faith. After the father's premature death, life became harder. To support her family, Agnes's mother set up a business selling cloth and embroidery. In her teens, Agnes became a member of a young people's group in her local parish called the Sodality. Through the activities there, guided by a Jesuit priest, Agnes became interested in the world of missionaries.

Her first call to a vocation as a Catholic missionary nun came when she was eighteen, and she chose to join an Irish order, the Sisters of Loreto, who were well known for their missionary work, particularly in India. From an early age she had wanted to work in India, but she went to Ireland first to learn English. On January 6, 1929, she was transferred to Calcutta to teach at St. Mary's High School. When she took her vows as a Sister of Loreto on May 24, 1931, she chose the name Teresa after St. Theresa of Lisieux, known as the Little Flower of Jesus.

Both the decision to leave her homeland and go to the other side of the world, and the choice of Teresa as her professed name, are essential clues to understanding Mother Teresa's strength, character, and purpose. They show her fervor for not just becoming religious, but wanting clearly to do missionary work—"to go out and give the life of Christ to the people" is how she refers to this first call.

The missionary life is one of zeal with a clear evangelistic thrust and a strong belief in compassion in action. Mother Teresa's pioneering spirit was there from the start. Yet missionary work is not only about compassionate action, and Mother Teresa gave a first sign of the contemplative side of her mission by picking St. Theresa of Lisieux as a saintly guide. The youngest daughter of a French watchmaker and his wife, Theresa entered the Carmelite order of sisters in 1888 at the very early age of fifteen, announcing that her vocation was "love" and that one of her principal duties was to pray for priests and missionaries. Unable herself, because of sickness, to be a missionary, she taught the ways of a healthy spirituality which was simple, full of generosity and sacrificial spirit, and oriented towards the essential truth of the Gospel. She wrote, "My little way is the way of spiritual childhood, the way of trust and absolute self-surrender." She likened herself to "a ball in the hands of the Child Jesus." Mother Teresa takes a less playful, more practical view of her simple way of trust and self-surrender, calling herself "a pencil in God's hands."

In Calcutta, Mother Teresa taught geography and catechism at St. Mary's and learned Hindi and Bengali; in 1944 she took over as principal of the school. It was a time of hardship—with food rationing and an increasing workload—and Mother Teresa, not a physically strong woman, succumbed to tuberculosis. She was unable to continue teaching and was sent to Darjeeling, in the foothills of the Himalayas.

It was on the train, on September 10, 1946, that she received her second call—"the call within the call," as she refers to it:

"And when that happens the only thing to do is to say 'Yes.' The message was quite clear—I was to give up all and follow Jesus into the slums—to serve Him in the poorest of the poor. I knew it was His will and that I had to follow Him. There was no doubt that it was to be His work. I was to leave the convent and work with the poor, living among them. It was an order. I knew where I belonged but I did not know how to get there."*

It took a couple of years to gain permission to redirect her missionary service from teacher to servant, from a secure and comfortable community to having nothing except exceptional faith and remarkable vision.

Many sisters who worked with Mother Teresa during her nineteen years at St. Mary's, when interviewed, spoke of the then Sister Teresa's fragile health

---

* Eileen Egan. *Such a Vision of the Street: Mother Teresa—The Spirit and the Work* (Garden City, NY: Doubleday, 1985), p. 25.

and ordinariness. Yet today, one could regard her as the quintessential, energetic entrepreneur, who has perceived a need and done something about it, built an organization against all odds, formulated its constitution, and sent out branches all over the world. And therein lies another example of the apparent anomalies within her character and her life. Mother Teresa is that rare combination of the grounded being and the transcendent soul, a combination brought about by prayer, which she says helps her strike "a proper balance between Earth and Heaven." This balance between a strong will and a complete surrender to God is instructive because she has said of her progress in holiness that "it depends on God and myself—on God's grace and my will. The first step to becoming is to will it."

Mother Teresa, when asked about her holiness or saintliness, always answers in a matter-of-fact way that holiness is a necessity in life—and explains that it is not the luxury of a few, such as those who take the course of religious life, but is "a simple duty of all. Holiness is for everyone."

The fact that she is called a living saint by many people may have to do with a concept that is becoming more and more prized in contemporary life: balance. The renowned Indian teacher Krishnamurti interpreted *holiness* as a derivative of "wholeness," meaning all the disparate parts of ourselves combined evenly into the whole person. Mother Teresa's spiritual path shows how important it is to balance the prayerful, contemplative life with the practical one of loving action. It is certainly simple, but behind Mother Teresa's simplicity are years of experience and devotion resulting in a faith and will and wisdom unsurpassed.

This balance between the awareness of the small details in the here and now and the larger, more eternal view allows her to be respectfully intimate, pragmatic yet perceptive, vulnerable yet strong, down-to-earth yet contemplative and prayerful. The following two stories illustrate her ability to be both generous and perceptive.

An English volunteer was deeply impressed when he first met Mother Teresa at his high school in his teens. "She could talk as well to us as to anybody. I think that was what impressed us, she was on our wavelength. This has continued to be with me at all times I have met her since. Whoever she's talking to, that person becomes the most important person in front of her. It doesn't matter if you're a president or Joe Soap. I like that and I think that most people who have met her feel that from her."

A woman who went to help the Missionaries of Charity in Calcutta and was pondering her own path met Mother Teresa by chance on the balcony outside her room at the Mother House. "She was just meeting a few people—there was an Indian couple before me and she suddenly turned round and looked at me and said, 'When will you make up your mind?' I was dumbstruck, and this was without me saying anything at all. She somehow knew who I was at a very deep level. It really moved me—she touched me and I spent the rest of the day in the chapel, crying and recovering. Then I knew I had to make the decision about my direction which I had been putting off for a very long time."

Because of the respect held for Mother Teresa internationally, a lot is expected of her.

If she is a woman, some ask, why then does she not become a spokesperson for the prominent women's issues, not only in the Church but also the world? Mother Teresa would certainly never deviate verbally from Church doctrine—she could not, nor would she probably want to. When asked about the burning issues of abortion and women priests, she is clear about her position that all human life is precious to God, with no exceptions, and she cites Mary, the Mother of Christ, when replying to the question of women's roles in high sacred duties. She says Mary would have made the best priest of us all; yet she called herself, and remained, the handmaid of the Lord. Mary is the role model for Mother Teresa and all the Missionaries of Charity, and is prayed to fervently as a symbol of great holiness, purity, chastity, surrender, and sacred motherhood. This feminine devotion to the divine mother is a woman's way to the heart of Christ. One of the prayers frequently recited by Mother Teresa and the Missionaries of Charity is:

Mary, Mother of Jesus, give me your heart, so beautiful, so pure, so immaculate, so full of love and humility, that I may be able to receive Jesus in the Bread of Life, love Him as you loved Him, and serve Him in the distressing disguise of the Poorest of the Poor.

This kind of service—to the poor—which Mother Teresa describes in detail in this book, isn't always about doing for the poor, but about being there in their suffering, sharing it with Christ. Mother Teresa frequently points out that, "That was what St. John and Our Blessed Mother were doing at the foot of the Cross."

Many of the Missionaries of Charity homes display large, sometimes gaudy statues of Mary dressed in blue and white, as she appeared to St. Bernadette at Lourdes, or as the Queen of Heaven haloed with stars and lights. Yet the signs of Mother Teresa's ecumenicism are often evident as well. For example, in Calcutta, just inside the gates of Prem Dan, the Missionaries of Charity home for TB and mentally handicapped patients, stands a life-size statue of the Madonna in a blue cape, holding Catholic rosary beads; yet at closer observation she has an Indian face, wears a white Indian tunic, and is held at her feet by a huge pink lotus blossom.

Many of the duties usually performed by priests, in the Benediction service for instance, and in parts of the daily Mass, are carried out by the sisters and Mother Teresa herself, and in general everyone gets on with serving God without too much limiting protocol.

Mother Teresa once said of herself: "By blood

and origin I am all Albanian. My citizenship is Indian. I am a Catholic nun. As to my calling, I belong to the whole world. As to my heart, I belong entirely to the heart of Jesus."* She defines her role in embracing the world by saying, "Our work is to encourage Christians and non-Christians to do works of love. And every work of love, done with a full heart, always brings people closer to God."** Her mandate of mercy is to spread love in the world by relieving the suffering of others—through a Catholic sisterhood and brotherhood who serve a largely non-Christian community, and who do not compel those they help to convert to the Catholic faith.

Mother Teresa has chosen to love where most people have not been able to, among the poor and the suffering. And it is there that she has found the fruits of her labor, and the steps for the simple path.

THE SIMPLE PATH

The Christian way has always been to love God and one's neighbor as oneself. Yet Mother Teresa has, perhaps with the influence of the East, distilled six steps to creating peace in ourselves and others that can be taken by anyone—even someone of no religious beliefs

* Eileen Egan. *Such a Vision of the Street*, p. 357.
** Ibid.

or of a religious background other than Christian—
with no insult to beliefs or practices. This is why,
when reading Mother Teresa's words and those of her
community, we may, if we choose, replace the references to Jesus with references to other godheads or
symbols of divinity.

However, Mother Teresa's chosen way is the
Christian one, and her divine guide is Jesus Christ.
Her commitment to Christ is central to all that she
and the other Missionaries of Charity do. As well as
their vows of poverty, obedience, and wholehearted
service to the poorest of the poor, both the men and
the women of the order take a vow of chastity,
through which the women become vowed and dedi-
cated to Christ while the men's hearts are free to be
"more inflamed with love for God and all men."*
Mother Teresa (and each of her sisters) refers to herself
as "Christ's spouse"; each sister is called to enter into
this relationship for the rest of her life, to love Jesus
with her whole heart. Mother Teresa has commented
on this relationship as a love that is similar to the love
of a wife for her husband: "We are all women who
have the ability to make use of this love. We should
not be ashamed of loving Jesus with our emotions."
She once responded to the many comments she'd received from people saying that she must be married to
have such wisdom about love in relationships, "Yes I
am, but sometimes I find it difficult to smile at Him

* Eileen Egan. *Such a Vision of the Street*, p. 307.

because He can be so demanding!" This dedication to God through the vow of chastity needs to be understood as central to the life of any religious sister. The person taking the vow renounces the married state in life and becomes consecrated to God. The commitment is more extreme than marriage, because the love given to others only happens through the love of God. "I cannot in conscience love a creature with the love of a woman for a man," Mother Teresa once said. "I no longer have the right to give that affection to any other creature but God."

The Missionaries of Charity sisters who contributed to this book shared some stories of their call to this particular life and vow. One said: "I used to read about Mother Teresa and her work. My faith was very deep and I believed in the words of the Bible, 'Whatever you did to the least of my brethren, you did it to me.' As a child I thought that this was to be my life and as I grew up I realized that this is the path I could take where I could do more and more for Jesus. It was a clear and immediate call because I knew here I could do that work for Christ, give every moment of my life for others." Another sister said: "Whatever I do, I do it for Jesus. Otherwise it is worthless, useless. So when I know I am doing it for Him, I can do it more lovingly, more compassionately towards the people who are suffering. It gives a lot of meaning to my life to know I am doing it for Him, and day after day this meaning increases."

In the Constitution of the Missionaries of Charity, this commitment to Christ is referred to as "A Bond of Love a Thousand Times Stronger Than Those of Flesh and Blood." So it is in this oneness, and through this bond, that Mother Teresa and the Missionaries of Charity pray, love, work, and share in their community. And it is from this bond of deep love that the steps on their simple path are taken in poverty and to relieve suffering. Christ not only loved in this world, but He showed His love through His suffering on the Cross. Mother Teresa's modus operandi is to relieve Christ's suffering as she sees it in the eyes of all who are poor and who suffer. Above all the crucifixes in the chapels of the Missionaries of Charity worldwide are the words "I thirst"—which is what Christ said before He died—and these words remind the missionaries of the implications of everything they do. As their constitution states: "Our aim is to quench the infinite thirst of Jesus Christ on the Cross for love of souls. We serve Jesus in the poor, we nurse Him, feed Him, clothe Him, visit Him."

The definition of poverty is broad in Mother Teresa's terms. She defines "least of my brethren" as "the hungry and the lonely, not only for food but for the Word of God; the thirsty and the ignorant, not only for water but also for knowledge, peace, truth, justice, and love; the naked and the unloved, not only for clothes but also for human dignity; the unwanted, the unborn child; the racially discriminated against; the homeless and abandoned, not only for a shelter made of bricks, but for a heart that understands, that covers, that loves; the sick, the dying destitutes, and the captives, not only in body but also in mind and spirit: all those who have lost all hope and faith in life, the alcoholics and drug addicts and all those who have lost God (for them God was but God is) and who have lost all hope in the power of the Spirit."

A volunteer priest who once helped the sisters in Calcutta said of the poor: "They are the ones who have nothing to prove or to protect—no posing, no posturing before people or before God. When all you've got is all you've got, all that's left is to be yourself and you can only receive. And that, in a sense, is why the poor are blessed, because they know what really matters."

To serve the poor, to allow them to receive, a certain losing of self is essential. Mother Teresa explains the necessity of poverty in her life as the condition of the work.* "How can you truly know the poor unless you live like them?" she asks. "If they complain about the food, we can say that we eat the same. The more we have the less we can give. Poverty is a wonderful gift because it gives us freedom—it means we have fewer obstacles to God." This is why when Missionaries of Charity are offered hospitality, they refuse. "The poor in their hovels and slums are seldom offered anything, so out of respect and empathy for them, we, too, always refuse."

* Omer Tanghe. *For the Least of My Brothers: The Spirituality of Mother Teresa & Catherine Doherty* (New York: Alba, 1989).

Just as a certain state of poverty is necessary to love and serve, so is "doing little things with great love." "It is simple but not easy," Mother Teresa states, and then goes on to explain the suffering that usually accompanies such deeds. There are five sufferings—physical, mental, emotional, financial, and spiritual—and any or all of these come into play at some point, whether you are the suffering recipient of love or the giver of love to the sufferer. All suffering is perceived as a sacrifice. Mother Teresa uses such phrases as "Love until it hurts" and "If it hurts, then it'll be better because of it." She believes that through understanding and willingly accepting the pain one is able to see its ultimate worth. This idea is connected with the redemption of the suffering Christ:

"Jesus wanted to help by sharing our life, our loneliness, our agony, our death. Only by being one with us has He redeemed us. We are allowed to do the same: all the desolation of the poor people, not only their material poverty, but their spiritual destitution, must be redeemed, and we must share it, for only by being one with them can we redeem them, that is, by bringing God into their lives and bringing them to God."*

This sharing of suffering, of poverty through acts of love and kindness, is the basis of the missionary

* M. Muggeridge. *Something Beautiful for God* (San Francisco: Harper & Row, 1971), pp. 67–68.

work of the Missionaries of Charity. "Without our suffering our work would be just social work."* It is the acceptance of suffering—not in a stoic, sacrificial way but with gladness of spirit—that brings joy into the work of these sisters and brothers. "What's the use of grumbling," says Mother Teresa. "If you accept suffering and offer it to God, that gives you joy. Suffering is a great gift of God; those who accept it willingly, those who love deeply, those who offer themselves know its value."**

Mother Teresa invites us to know poverty and suffering and to experience the joy of giving and receiving, not just by reading this book, but by living and sharing the work. It is through the experience of contact that we can all know the truth of her words, and the words of others who have trod the path—and this contact can be made at any point in the six steps. It is a contact of intimacy, of faith, of belief, of the heart, and of grace, and is sustained through its fruits. These fruits Mother Teresa has experienced time and time again. Through her words and her work we can know these fruits for ourselves, we can accomplish something extraordinary by doing something ordinary with love—"just one day at a time."

LUCINDA VARDEY, 1995

* M. Muggeridge. *Something Beautiful for God*, pp.67–68.
** Edward Le Joly. *We Do It for Jesus: Mother Teresa and Her Missionaries of Charity* (Queens Village, NY: Oxford University Press, 1977).

BEFORE
READING
ON

An Indian admirer of Mother Teresa, a business-man, once had five lines (shown on page 1) printed for her on small yellow cards. These she calls her "business cards" and she offers them freely to people because they clearly explain the direction of her work, her simple path. This path is one that she has distilled from her long experience of working for the love of God with her fellow human beings. It is composed of six essential steps: silence, prayer, faith, love, service, and peace. Familiarity with one will naturally lead on to another. If one surrenders to the nature of the process, life will inevitably run more smoothly, more joyfully, and more peacefully.

Over the years, men and women have felt inspired to join Mother Teresa in her work. They have taken the vows of poverty, chastity, obedience, and wholehearted free service to the poorest of the poor and have undergone a long training to become senior members of the Missionaries of Charity. This Order was set up by Mother Teresa; its members have been trained by her and with her support. Thus, the work and attitudes of the nuns and monks who speak in this book are informed by Mother Teresa's simple philosophy.

This catching force, fanning out in ever-increasing circles, can also be found in the experiences of the volunteers who have helped the Missionaries of Charity throughout the world. By working alongside the sisters and brothers, they too have absorbed Mother Teresa's approach to life. They both live it and, in many cases, have recast it in the particular conditions of the West. Thus their testimonies are also valuable and inspiring.

By contemplating and practicing some of the many thoughts and suggestions in this book, we, too, can discover the benefits of the simple path—and we don't necessarily have to be Catholics, or specifically religious, to do so. There are numerous practical strategies in the following pages that we can try out for ourselves in our own communities. If we find silence or prayer unfamiliar and we are not sure if we believe in anything very much, then Mother Teresa suggests we try offering small acts of love to others—and we will find our hearts will open. The important thing is that, having read, we should *do* something, anything, and by that act of love we (and others) will be enriched.

THE SIMPLE PATH

The fruit of silence is
PRAYER.
The fruit of prayer is
FAITH.
The fruit of faith is
LOVE.
The fruit of love is
SERVICE.
The fruit of service is
PEACE.

PRAYER

✦

THE
FRUIT
OF
SILENCE
IS
PRAYER

We all must take the time to be silent and to contemplate, especially those who live in big cities like London and New York, where everything moves so fast. This is why I decided to open our first home for contemplative sisters (whose vocation is to pray most of the day) in New York instead of the Himalayas: I felt silence and contemplation were needed more in the cities of the world.

I always begin my prayer in silence, for it is in the silence of the heart that God speaks. God is the friend of silence—we need to listen to God because it's not what we say but what He says to us and through us that matters. Prayer feeds the soul—as blood is to the body, prayer is to the soul—and it brings you closer to God. It also gives you a clean and pure heart. A clean heart can see God, can speak to God, and can see the love of God in others. When you have a clean heart it means you are open and honest with God, you are not hiding anything from Him, and this lets Him take what He wants from you.

If you are searching for God and do not know where to begin, learn to pray and take the trouble to pray every day. You can pray anytime, anywhere. You do not have to be in a chapel or a church. You can pray at work—work doesn't have to stop prayer and prayer doesn't have to stop work. You can also consult a priest or minister for guidance, or try speaking directly to God. Just speak. Tell Him everything, talk to Him. He is our father, He is father to us all whatever religion we are. We are all created by God, we are his children. We have to put our trust in Him and love Him, believe in Him, work for Him. And if we pray, we will get all the answers we need.

Without prayer I could not work for even half an hour. I get my strength from God through prayer, which is something all the sisters understand, including Sister Dolores, who has been with our Order for thirty-five years and now runs Nirmal Hriday, the home for the dying and destitute in Calcutta:

"Every morning the sisters wake up knowing what they have to go through again, which is sometimes very difficult for them. Prayer gives them strength—it sustains, helps, and gives us all the joy to carry out what we need to do. We begin the day with prayer and with Mass and we end the day with an hour of Adoration before Jesus. To continuously do and to continuously give needs God's graces—without them it would be impossible for us to live."

Also, Sister Charmaine Jose, who is in charge of the children's home, Shishu Bhavan, in Calcutta says:

"I don't know how we could face this heat and this busy work without prayer, but the work is entirely for Him so we are happy to do it."

Sister Kateri, a Superior Sister in our home in the Bronx, New York, explains this through her own experience:

"The most important thing that a human being can do is pray, because we've been made for God and our hearts are restless until we rest with Him. And it's in prayer that we come into contact with God. We are made for Heaven and we're not going to get to Heaven if we don't pray in *some* way. It doesn't necessarily have to be formal prayer.

"I used to share this with the men at the prison I visited. I'd give them the example: If you had to go on a trip, what would you need? And the men would say, 'You'd need a car and you'd need gasoline.' (One man said, 'Music'!) We used to have a good time because we usually decided that the gasoline was prayer, the car was our life, the journey was to heaven, you had to have a map, you had to know where you were going, and so on. My point really is that the gasoline of our life is prayer and without that we won't reach our destination, and we won't reach the fulfillment of our being."

HOW
TO
PRAY:
A
SIMPLE
CONTACT
WITH
GOD

❦

S tart and end the day with prayer. Come to God as a child. If you find it hard to pray you can say, "Come Holy Spirit, guide me, protect me, clear out my mind so that I can pray." Or, if you pray to Mary, you can say, "Mary, Mother of Jesus, be a mother to me now, help me to pray."

When you pray, give thanks to God for all His gifts because everything is His and a gift from Him. Your soul is a gift of God. If you are Christian, you can say the Lord's Prayer; if Catholic, the Our Father, the Hail Mary, the Rosary, the Creed—all common prayers. If you or your family have your own devotions, then pray according to them.

If you trust in the Lord and the power of prayer you will overcome any feelings of doubt and fear and loneliness that people commonly feel.

If there is something that is worrying you, then you can go to Confession (if you are a Catholic) and become perfectly clean, because Jesus forgives everything through the priest. It is a beautiful gift of God that we may go to Confession full of sin and come out perfectly pure. However, whether you go to Confession or not, or whether you are Catholic or from another religion, you should at least know how to say "Sorry" to God.

Every night before you go to bed you must make an examination of conscience (because you don't know if you will be alive in the morning!). Whatever is troubling you, or whatever wrong you may have done, you need to repair it. For example, if you have stolen something, then try to give it back. If you have hurt somebody, try to make up to that person; do it directly. If you cannot make up like that, at least then make up with God by saying, "I'm very sorry." This is important because just as we have acts of love, we also must have acts of contrition. You could say, "Lord, I'm sorry for having offended you and I promise you I will try not to offend you again," something like this. It feels good to be free of burdens, to have a clean heart. Remember that God is merciful, He is the merciful father to us all. We are His children and He will forgive and forget if we remember to do so.

Examine your heart first, though, to see if there is any lack of forgiveness of others still inside, because how can we ask God for forgiveness if we cannot forgive others? Remember, if you truly repent, if you really mean it with a clean heart, you will be absolved in God's eyes. He will forgive you if you truly confess. So pray to be able to forgive those who have hurt you or whom you don't like, and forgive as you have been forgiven.

You can also pray for the work of others and help them. For example, in our community there are "second self" helpers who offer their prayers for a sister who needs the strength to carry on her active work. And we also have the contemplative sisters and brothers, who pray for us all the time.

There are so many stories about the power of prayer and how God always answers us. A priest, Father Bert White, visited us in Calcutta because he was interested in our work. He came at just the right time:

"I was on my way to see the work of Mother Teresa and the Missionaries of Charity and decided to attend Mass at the Mother House. Arriving at the front door, I was greeted by a sister who said to me, 'Thank God you're here, Father, come on in.' I said, 'How do you know I'm a priest?' because I was not wearing my clerical clothes, and she answered, 'The priest who usually says Mass couldn't come so we prayed to God to send us another.' "

MAKE
YOUR
FAMILY
A
FAMILY
OF
LOVE

❧

Prayer is needed for children and in families. Love begins at home and that is why it is important to pray together. If you pray together you will stay together and love each other as God loves each one of you. Whatever religion we are, we must pray together. Children need to learn to pray and they need to have their parents pray with them. If we don't do this, it will be difficult to become holy, to carry on, to strengthen ourselves in faith.

Sister Theresina, the Regional Superior for the British Isles and Ireland, shares her experience of this:

"It is from the family that the child is supposed to get the first spiritual formation, and within the family it is meant to be nurtured and to grow. This is not happening much at all now. The majority of parents we come into contact with have lost their faith and therefore have lost any kind of dependence on God. They are deprived of all the gifts that God can give them to raise their children properly; they are deprived of the wisdom and the discernment to guide their children when needed. Many parents say to me, 'I'm sorry, I just can't control my children, they are out of control.' "

There is so much suffering in families these days all over the world that it is important to pray, and it is important to forgive. People ask me what advice I have for a married couple struggling in their relationship. I always answer "Pray and forgive"; and to young people who come from violent homes, "Pray and forgive"; and to the single mother with no family support, "Pray and forgive." You can say, "My Lord, I love You. My God, I am sorry. My God, I believe in You. My God, I trust You. Help us to love one another as You love us."

We pray to the Holy Family (Mary, Joseph, and Jesus) for our family. We say:

Heavenly Father, You have given us a model of life in the Holy Family of Nazareth. Help us, O loving Father, to make our family another Nazareth where love, peace, and joy reign.

May it be deeply contemplative, intensely Eucharistic, and vibrant with joy.

Help us to stay together in joy and sorrow through family prayer.

Teach us to see Jesus in the members of our family, especially in His distressing disguises.

May the Eucharistic Heart of Jesus make our hearts meek and humble like His and help us to carry out our family duties in a holy way.

May we love one another as God loves each one of us more and more each day, and forgive each other's faults as You forgive our sins.

Help us, O loving Father, to take whatever You give and to give whatever You take with a big smile.

Immaculate Heart of Mary, cause of our joy, pray for us.

Saint Joseph pray for us.

Holy Guardian Angels be always with us, guide and protect us.

Amen.

GOD

IS

A

FRIEND

OF

SILENCE

❧

We all need time for silence, to reflect and to pray. Many people tell me how difficult it is to find silence in their busy lives.

First Sister Theresina and then Sister Kateri offer their comments and advice on this:

"From what I have found, there is just too much noise in modern life—and because of this many people are afraid of silence. As God speaks only in silence, this is a big problem for those searching for God. Many young people, for instance, don't know how to reflect and just act instinctively.

"In cities these days there is so much chaos and physical violence, a lot of anger, frustration, and shouting, just the opposite of the peaceful countryside or

the sound of a waterfall. People try to fill the emptiness they feel with food, radio, television, and keeping
busy with outside activities. But this emptiness can
only be filled by the spiritual, by God. If we give time
for God to enter this space, then our hunger can be
more easily satisfied by just being with God in prayer.
From this place we can grow stronger in our relationship with God and in our spiritual life. But it is a hard
thing to be prayerful in our society, which feeds us
with so many distractions."

"As a Missionaries of Charity sister I don't have
many opportunities to be alone. Choosing a life of
poverty usually means a lack of privacy—we don't
have our own rooms to pray and contemplate alone.
However, once I did have the opportunity to be alone
for a day and the first thing I really wanted to do was
to read—I love books and I am usually so busy I forget to read as much as I'd like. The book I found,
which was a gift from God as it was just the book I
needed to read, was a collection of writings by St.
Catherine of Siena. She had been in the same quan-
dary back in fourteenth-century Italy—trying to pray
and be silent as she grew up in a household of twenty-
five children. She wrote about how each of us needs to
find a 'cell' within ourselves where we go to pray and
to be with God. Her point was that most of us cannot
go off into the mountains and be a hermit in a cave,
so we must discover this special place within. I believe
we can and need to do as she advises. Among all the

other duties in life we still need to learn to pray and to be able to find an atmosphere of silence even in the middle of a noisy home or city.

"When I used to make my weekly visits to the local prison, I witnessed the people there who hungered and thirsted for this silent place. We usually spent time praying together, and it was so beautiful to see tough men—many of whom had killed others and lived hard, tough lives—bow their heads like children and pray sincerely. I knew that once they came into an atmosphere of some kind of silence, they would just fall into a peaceful state."

And Sister Dolores offers this advice:

"If everyone in the world took five or ten minutes daily to stop and think, it would help us all to go about God's work, because we need reflection, we need to ask God for His blessing daily, and we need to bring Him into our lives so we can give Him to others. When we have God in our lives it brings meaning into them, it makes everything worthwhile and fruitful, too. The absence of God usually accompanies the less-than-perfect things in our world."

EQUAL
BEFORE
GOD

There is only one God and He is God to all; therefore it is important that everyone is seen as equal before God. I've always said we should help a Hindu become a better Hindu, a Muslim become a better Muslim, a Catholic become a better Catholic.

Brother Vinod, who runs Gandhiji Prem Nivas, our center for leprosy patients in Titagarh, Calcutta, understands how we try not to preach religion, but just to show our faith through our actions and our dedication, as does Sister Theresina in London:

"We believe our work should be our example to people. We have among us 475 souls—30 families are Catholics and the rest are all Hindus, Muslims, Sikhs— all different religions. But they all come to our prayers.

At seven o'clock everyone assembles for thirty minutes. And we have readings—some Bible and other
scriptures—any book can be read. A patient sometimes
will give a small oration."

"I have never found a problem with people from
different religions praying together. What I have found
is that people are just hungry for God, and be they
Christian or Muslim we invite them to pray with us.
There is a large percentage of Muslims in our mission
houses in Spain and France and they want to pray. So
that is our main focus, to encourage them to pray, to
have a relationship with God, however that may be,
because when you have that then everything else will
follow."

PRAY
EVERY
DAY

❧

Try to feel the need for prayer often during the day and take the trouble to pray. Prayer makes the heart large enough until it can contain God's gift of Himself. Ask and seek, and your heart will grow big enough to receive Him and keep Him as your own.

The following are prayers that we say every day from our prayerbook. I hope they may be helpful if you do not know any prayers, or would like to know more. You could replace "Jesus" by "God" if you are not a Christian.

❧

Let us all become a true and fruitful branch on the vine Jesus, by accepting Him in our lives as it pleases Him to come:

as the Truth—to be told;
as the Life—to be lived;
as the Light—to be lighted;
as the Love—to be loved;
as the Way—to be walked;
as the Joy—to be given;
as the Peace—to be spread;
as the Sacrifice—to be offered,
in our families and within our neighborhood.

O God, we believe You are here.
We adore and love You with our whole heart and soul
because You are most worthy of all our love.
We desire to love You as the Blessed do in Heaven.
We adore all the designs of Your divine Providence,
resigning ourselves entirely to Your Will.
We also love our neighbor for Your sake as we love
ourselves.
We sincerely forgive all who have injured us, and ask
pardon of all whom we have injured.
Dear Jesus, help us to spread Your fragrance every-
where we go.
Flood our souls with Your spirit and life.
Penetrate and possess our whole being, so utterly,
That our lives may only be a radiance of Yours.
Shine through us, and be so in us,
That every soul we come in contact with may feel
Your presence in our soul.
Let them look up and see no longer us, but only Jesus!

Stay with us, and then we shall begin to shine as You
  shine;
So to shine as to be a light to others.
The light O Jesus will be all from You, none of it will
  be ours;
It will be You, shining on others through us.
Let us thus praise You in the way You love best by
  shining on those around us.
Let us preach You without preaching, not by words
  but by our example,
By the catching force, the sympathetic influence of
  what we do,
The evident fullness of the love our hearts bear to You.
Amen.

Deliver me, O Jesus,
From the desire of being loved,
From the desire of being extolled,
From the desire of being honored,
From the desire of being praised,
From the desire of being preferred,
From the desire of being consulted,
From the desire of being approved,
From the desire of being popular,
From the fear of being humiliated,
From the fear of being despised,
From the fear of suffering rebukes,
From the fear of being calumniated,
From the fear of being forgotten,

From the fear of being wronged,
From the fear of being ridiculed,
From the fear of being suspected.

FAITH

THE
FRUIT
OF
PRAYER
IS
FAITH

G od is everywhere and in everything and without Him we cannot exist. I have never for one moment doubted the existence of God but I know some people do. If you don't believe in God you can help others by doing works of love, and the fruit of these works are the extra graces that come into your soul. Then you'll begin to slowly open up and want the joy of loving God.

There are so many religions and each one has its different ways of following God. I follow Christ:
Jesus is my God,
Jesus is my Spouse,
Jesus is my Life,
Jesus is my only Love,
Jesus is my All in All,
Jesus is my Everything.

Because of this I am never afraid. I am doing my work with Jesus, I'm doing it for Jesus, I'm doing it to Jesus, and therefore the results are His, not mine. If you need a guide, you only have to look to Jesus. You have to surrender to Him and rely on Him completely. When you do this, all doubt is dispelled and you are filled with conviction. Jesus said, "Unless you become a child you cannot come to me."

Sister Theresina explains it like this:

"We are working for the Kingdom, we have devoted our lives to the Kingdom of God, so He definitely has to be the one who guides us and leads us and provides for us. For instance, we never lose sight of God's providence, so we try not to store the things that we need, and just to manage with whatever comes as it comes. I think in this way we will continue to receive God's blessings, especially if we don't become extravagant and if we don't get caught up in living for the future, instead of right now in the present. We need to be flexible—when it is God's time things are easy and when it's not His time things are difficult. We must really listen to the invitation that God extends to us in whichever way it is manifested."

Here, Sister Kateri describes how it feels to entrust your life to God:

"There is a certain freedom in really trusting in God's providence. We try to live in the present and not to worry about tomorrow, although making plans is certainly part of being responsible. Where others would plan a year in advance, we would never do that. And sometimes when people would never consider doing something because it wasn't planned in advance, we would do it without another thought. Our approach would be to at least try—and so often it works out."

Let Jesus use you without consulting you. We let Him take what He wants from us. So take whatever He gives and give whatever He takes with a big smile. Accept the gifts of God and be deeply grateful. If He has given you great wealth, make use of it, try to share it with others, with those who don't have anything. Always share with others because even with a little help you may save them from becoming distressed. And don't take more than you need, that's all. Just accept whatever comes.

The sisters in New York have been given great help over the years by a dentist called Mark. He once told us the following story, which illustrates my point about acceptance:

"I trust that things are perfect just the way they are: the problems are in the way I observe them. I remember once I was talking to one of the sisters, my wife was pregnant and she was having difficulties and was going to have a miscarriage. My immediate thought was that I would pray that the baby would be OK. Then it dawned on me that that was the wrong prayer. The prayer should have been to be given the strength to accept what is in God's plan for us."

As Missionaries of Charity, we are here to help the poorest of the poor in whatever form that takes, which is always Christ in His distressing disguise. We don't accept even one rupee for the work we do, as we do our work for Jesus. He looks after us. If He wants something done, He gives us the means. If He doesn't provide us with the means, then He doesn't want that work done.

It is the same for everyone, whether Missionary of Charity or not, as Father Bert White comments:

"I think when you focus on money and property ownership, you go the way of the material world, of the Big, of Up and More. It becomes your agenda and then faith can fly out of the window. There has to be faith and a trust in God's reality—a trust that things will work out.

"There aren't two worlds—the physical and the spiritual—there's only one: God's Kingdom on Earth as it is in Heaven. Many of us pray, 'Our Father, who art in Heaven,' thinking that God is up there, which creates the duality of the two worlds. A lot of people in the West like to keep matter and the spirit very comfortably and conveniently apart. All truth is one, all reality is one. As soon as we take the enfleshment of God, the incarnation which, for Christians, is represented by the person of Jesus Christ, then we start taking things seriously."

GOD'S
TEST
FOR
US

❧

We are all capable of good and evil. We are not born bad: everybody has something good inside. Some hide it, some neglect it, but it is there. God created us to love and to be loved, so it is our test from God to choose one path or the other. Any negligence in loving can lead someone to say Yes to evil, and when that happens we have no idea how far it can spread. That's the sad part. If someone chooses evil, then an obstacle is set up between that person and God, and the burdened person cannot see God clearly at all. That's why we have to avoid any kind of temptation that will destroy us. We gain the strength to overcome this from prayer, because if we are close to God we spread joy and love to everybody around us.

If evil takes possession of someone, that person, in turn, may spread evil to everybody around him. If we are in contact with such people we must try and help them and show them that God cares for them. Pray hard to help bring prayer back to them so that they may once more see God in themselves and then see Him in others. It is this which will help the person who is bad because everybody—it doesn't matter who—has been created by the same loving hand. Christ's love is always stronger than the evil in the world, so we need to love and to be loved: it's as simple as that. This shouldn't be such a struggle to achieve.

EACH
LIFE
IS
PRECIOUS
TO
GOD

☙

Unborn children are among the poorest of the poor. They are so close to God. I always ask doctors at hospitals in India never to kill an unborn child. If there is no one who wants it, I'll take it.

I see God in the eyes of every child—every unwanted child is welcomed by us. We then find homes for these children through adoption.

You know, people worry all the time about innocent children being killed in wars, and they try to prevent this. But what hope is there in stopping it if mothers kill their own children? Every life is precious to God, whatever the circumstances. In Isaiah, chapter 43, verse 4, God says, "You are precious to me and I love you."

We teach natural family planning to the poor in our many centers around the world. Women are given beads so that they can count the days in their cycle. A husband and wife should love and respect each other to be able to practice self-control during the fertile days.

As Sister Dolores says, these things are for God to decide:

"Since we believe that each one of us is unique and precious before God, then it is He who will be alongside us in our lives and as we go about doing our work. He is the boss and He tells us what to do. It is all very simple but sometimes we put Him aside and think we are the ones in charge."

THE
CHURCH
IS
OUR
FAMILY

~

G od is not separate from the Church as He is everywhere and in everything and we are all His children—Hindu, Muslim, or Christian. When we gather in His name this gives us strength. The Church gives us our priests, the Mass, and the Sacraments, which we need in our daily lives to do our work. We need the Eucharist (Jesus in the Host and Holy Communion) because unless we are given Jesus we cannot give to Him.

The Church is our family and like any family we need to be able to live together. Bishops invite the Missionaries of Charity to open new homes all the time and often help us find the houses. I do not see being a Catholic and belonging to the Catholic Church as a restriction: we just need to love and understand each other. I get asked about my opinions on the role of the Church today, on women's place within it, and what the future holds, and I say I don't have time to worry about all these issues—there are too many things to do in my everyday work. We are serving Christ. In our house He is head of our family and He makes all the decisions. For Christ, the Church is the same yesterday, today, and tomorrow. To God, everything is simple—God's love for us is greater than all the conflicts, which will pass.

FAITH

IS

A

GIFT

OF

GOD

❧

*I*t is God's wish that we grow in our faith, as Sister Theresina explains:

"Our faith is meant to grow and to mature. There are people who are perhaps very well educated, yet their faith is still at the first-grade level, and they don't find any meaning in the world. They have probably never read Scripture, never got to know God, never really got to know the beautiful person that He is—and so they look at God a little suspiciously. To them, he's like the judge or the very strict father who doesn't want them to have any fun."

Here, Sister Kateri expands on the nature of faith itself:

"Our understanding of 'faith' as Catholics is that it is a supernatural virtue infused in the soul. It's as if this virtue is a power, an ability. For example, if we didn't have legs we wouldn't be able to walk. If we didn't have eyes we wouldn't be able to see. Without faith, we are not able to believe in things that are mysteries and that are beyond our capacity to comprehend. You can't *understand* the mysteries of faith—but they should make sense. As we grow into adulthood, we need to penetrate them, to understand them more, so that it becomes more and more credible.

"Faith is a gift of God and grows through prayer, as do hope and love—and those are the three main virtues of the interior life."

Living a Christian life provides for the growth of faith. There have been many saints who have gone before to guide us, but I like the ones who are simple, like St. Theresa of Lisieux, the Little Flower of Jesus. I chose her as my namesake because she did ordinary things with extraordinary love.

It is good to study and read the works of the saints and other holy people (one of my favorite books is Seeds of the Desert *by Charles de Foucauld), but we find that God teaches us all we need to learn through our actions and our work, as Sister Dolores explains:*

"We do try and take the time for spiritual reading: I love to read the works of the saints, which have been helpful, and anything on our Blessed Mother, Our Lady—she is the best of mothers. But we don't have a lot of time to sit down. We celebrate different feast days, like those of St. Francis and St. Theresa, and September 10, when God spoke to Mother on the train to Darjeeling, telling her to serve the poorest of the poor. But really I don't need to read many books because I am being taught all the time by others. The AIDS patients I worked with in New York and Washington are the modern saints, the new saints of the Church. As they grew in Jesus, their last days, hours, and moments were so beautiful that for me theirs are the stories of the saints."

At the same time, it is important to gain self-knowledge as part of spiritual growth—to know yourself and believe in yourself means you can know and believe in God. St. Augustine said, "Fill yourselves first and then only will you be able to give to others." Knowledge of yourself produces humility, and knowledge of God produces love—as Sister Kateri describes:

"As one grows in prayer one grows also in the knowledge of oneself and if not in one's sinfulness, then certainly in potential sinfulness. It brings about a real understanding of what St. Philip Neri said, 'There go I, but for the grace of God.' And, as time goes on, it's much easier to accept the weaknesses of others because deep down there is at least the potential for sinfulness in oneself—we are all human, we all have the same human weakness."

THE
TREES
OF
SELF-DEFEAT
AND
SELF-
REALIZATION

❧

THE TREE OF SELF-DEFEAT

In the branches: Emptiness   Alienation   Apathy
Interpersonal Conflicts   Crime
Dependency   Alcoholism
Drug Addiction

In the roots: Fear   Insecurity   Resentment
Jealousy   Mistrust   Hostility
Guilt   Self-Pity

THE TREE OF SELF-REALIZATION

In the branches: Purposefulness   Health   Joy
Self-Motivation   Contentment
Acceptance   Fulfillment
Creativity

In the roots: Charity   Friendship   Forgiveness
Love   Gratitude   Kindness
Warmth   Trust

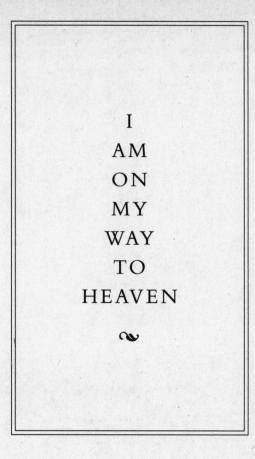

I
AM
ON
MY
WAY
TO
HEAVEN

From a sign on the morgue of the home for the dying and destitute, Calcutta

All things are decided by God. He decides when we live and when we die. We have to put our faith in Him and do the work that He has called us to do right up to when we die, as Sister Dolores explains:

"Every day is a preparation for death. By realizing this, it helps somehow, because what the dying go through today, I will go through tomorrow. We have to learn to live our days in union with Him. Death is nothing except going back to Him, where He is and where we all belong."

Anyone is capable of going to Heaven. Heaven is our home. People ask me about death and whether I look forward to it and I answer, "Of course," because I am going home. Dying is not the end, it is just the begin-

ning. Death is a continuation of life. This is the meaning of eternal life; it is where our soul goes to God, to
be in the presence of God, to see God, to speak to
God, to continue loving Him with greater love because in Heaven we shall be able to love Him with our
whole heart and our soul. We only surrender our body
in death—our heart and our soul live forever.

When we die we are going to be with God, and
with all those we have known who have gone before
us: our family and our friends will be there waiting for
us. Heaven must be a beautiful place.

Every religion has an eternity, another life.
People who fear death are the ones who believe this is
the end. I have not known anyone to die in fear if that
person has witnessed the love of God. The person has
to make peace with God, as do we all. People die suddenly all the time, so it could happen to us too at any
moment. Yesterday is gone and tomorrow has not yet
come; we must live each day as if it were our last so
that when God calls us we are ready, and prepared, to
die with a clean heart.

LOVE

THE
FRUIT
OF
FAITH
IS
LOVE

The greatest disease in the West today is not TB or leprosy; it is being unwanted, unloved, and uncared for. We can cure physical diseases with medicine, but the only cure for loneliness, despair, and hopelessness is love. There are many in the world who are dying for a piece of bread but there are many more dying for a little love. The poverty in the West is a different kind of poverty—it is not only a poverty of loneliness but also of spirituality. There's a hunger for love, as there is a hunger for God.

It is impossible to respond to this need unless you have God's grace to help you. First Sister Dolores and then Sister Kateri explain this further:

"We must be loved by God first, and only then can we give to others. For us to want to give love to others we must be full of love to give. God acts in this way. It is He who moves us all to do what we are doing, and if we feel His love for us then this love emanates from us. His love has no boundaries."

"There is only one love and this is the love of God. Once we love God deeply enough we will love our neighbor to the same extent because, as we grow in our love for God, we grow to respect all that He has created and to recognize and appreciate all the gifts He has given us. Then naturally we want to take care of all of them.

"God made the world for the delight of human beings—if only we could see His goodness everywhere, His concern for us, His awareness of our needs: the phone call we've waited for, the ride we are offered, the letter in the mail, just the little things He does for us throughout the day. As we remember and notice His love for us, we just begin to fall in love with Him because He is so busy with us—you just can't resist Him. I believe there's no such thing as luck in life, it's God's love, it's His."

When you know how much God is in love with you then you can only live your life radiating that love. I always say that love starts at home: family first, and then your own town or city. It is easy to love people who are far away but it is not always so easy to love those who live with us or right next to us. I do not agree with the big way of doing things—love needs to start with an individual. To get to love a person, you must contact that person, become close. Everyone needs love. All must know that they're wanted and that they are important to God.

Jesus said, "Love one another as I have loved you." He also said, "Whatever you did to the least of my brethren, you did it to me," so we love Him in the poor. He said, "I was hungry and you fed me . . . I was naked and you clothed me."

I always remind the sisters and brothers that our day is made up of twenty-four hours with Jesus. Sister Theresina explains this more; and then Father Bert White provides his views.

"We are contemplatives in the world and so our lives are centered on prayer and action. Our work is an outflow of our contemplation, our union with God in whatever we do, and through our work (which we call our Apostolate) we feed our union with God so that prayer and action and action and prayer are in continual flow."

"Gandhi said, 'Act, but seek not the fruit of your actions.' Your actions flow out of who you are, that's the fruit. It's a bit like being in love—when love just flows out to the person you are in love with."

The following prayer is the prayer every Missionary of Charity says before leaving for his or her Apostolate. It is also used as the Physician's Prayer in Shishu Bhavan, the children's home in Calcutta:

Dear Lord, the Great Healer, I kneel before You,
Since every perfect gift must come from You.
I pray, give skill to my hands, clear vision to my mind,
      kindness and meekness to my heart.
Give me singleness of purpose, strength to lift up a part
      of the burden of my suffering fellow men, and a
      true realization of the privilege that is mine.
Take from my heart all guile and worldliness,
That with the simple faith of a child, I may rely on You.

THE
WARMTH
OF
OUR
HAND

❧

L ove is not patronizing and charity isn't about pity, it is about love. Charity and love are the same—with charity you give love, so don't just give money but reach out your hand instead. When I was in London, I went to see the homeless people where our sisters have a soup kitchen. One man, who was living in a cardboard box, held my hand and said, "It's been a long time since I felt the warmth of a human hand."

Mary, one of our volunteers, has more ideas for reaching out to people:

"I've found that practical help can actually put people down unless it's done with love. No one wants to have things done for them, or be done to. I've also found trying to make contact with people has come in stages and that it has helped to do this in an organized way, like going to give the sisters a hand at the soup kitchen. Then it's best to try not to get too busy with giving out the food and clearing up the plates but to try to make a point of talking to somebody while you're there, or sitting down beside somebody—trying to make one-to-one contact. A lot of people carry photographs with them and so you can ask to see their photographs—or make a joke about their hairstyle—anything!

"The important thing is to find some point of contact even if it's just saying, "Did you enjoy your meal?" Instead of standing in the background doing the dishes, you can make sure you're the one who collects the plates. I think if you find this sort of thing difficult it's probably better to do it gradually—if you see somebody standing, or walking or sitting alone, then take the opportunity to reach out to them."

Here is a different story, also from Mary, that shows another way to make contact with people in need:

"A group of us went to Albania a while ago, and visited the sisters there. We heard about a home for handicapped children and so went to see them—but it was just a disaster. Apparently, the place had been given loads and loads of aid, but every time this happened, the people in the area came and ransacked it because they also needed things. Also, what struck me was that a lot of stuff was being flown in and there were warehouses packed full of aid—but it wasn't getting to people. So we went back with a box of apples and made a point of giving one to each child because we knew that if we just left the box, probably the other people around would also need the apples for their children too and the ones in the orphanage might not get them."

Love has no meaning if it isn't shared. Love has to be put into action. You have to love without expectation, to do something for love itself, not for what you may receive. If you expect something in return, then it isn't love, because true love is loving without conditions and expectations.

If there is a need God will guide you, as He guided us to serve those with AIDS. We don't judge these people, we don't ask what happened to them and how they got sick, we just see the need and care for them. I think God is telling us something with AIDS, giving us an opportunity to show our love. People with AIDS have awakened the tender love in those who had perhaps shut it out and forgotten it.

Sister Dolores shows how simply being there with love is often enough:

"There is a lot of fear at the beginning for those who come to us with AIDS. It is hard for them to cope with the fact that they are going to die. But being there with us and seeing us with others in their last moments makes a difference. I remember in New York that the mother of a man from Puerto Rico offered to nurse him if he came home. He thanked her but said he would remain with us, though he would visit her. One day he told me, 'I know when I am dying you will be there holding my hand,' because he had seen us doing it with others and knew that he wouldn't die alone.

"It's quite simple really. The dying are moved by the love they receive and it may be just a touch of my hand, or a glass of water, or providing them with some kind of sweet they desire. You just take that to them, what they ask for, and they are satisfied and know someone cares for them, someone loves them, someone wants them—and that, in itself, is a great help to them. Because of this they believe that God must be even kinder, more generous, and so their souls are lifted up to God. As we don't preach, we just do what we do with love, they are touched by God's grace."

Brother Geoff, General Servant of the Missionaries of Charity Brothers, also comments on the best way to offer love:

"When people who are used to being rejected and abandoned experience being accepted by others and being loved, when they see people are giving their time and energy for them, that conveys a message that, after all, they are not rubbish.

"Certainly, love is expressed first in being *with* before doing *to* someone. We have to continually renew our awareness of this because we can get caught up in a lot of the doing for. You see, if our actions do not first come from the desire to be with a person, then it really becomes just social work. When you are willing to be with a poor person you can recognize his need and if your love is genuine you naturally want to do what you can as an expression of your love. Service, in a way, is simply a means of expressing your being *for* that person—and often with the poorest people you cannot completely alleviate their problem. But by being with them, by being for them, whatever you can do for them makes a difference. The message we try to convey to the poorest of the poor is: We cannot solve your problems but God loves you even while you are handicapped or alcoholic or have leprosy, and whether or not you become cured, God loves you just as much and we are here to express that love. And if we can help relieve their pain a bit all well and good, but it is more important for us to remind them that even in the midst of pain and suffering, God loves them. It's a difficult message to communicate, obviously, but we believe that being for them is the first thing. If you spend time with a person then that is as much an expression of love as what you can do for them."

Here, one of our volunteers, Nigel, describes his experience at our home for the dying and destitute in Calcutta:

"When I went to help at Nirmal Hriday I hated the place because of the suffering, and I felt absolutely useless. I thought, What am I doing here?

"Later, when I got back to Britain, I had a long conversation with one of the sisters about it. I told her I'd quickly learned sign language so I could sort out the difference between someone asking for a drink of water or for a bedpan and get it the right way round. But, apart from that, I hadn't done a lot. I mostly sat on people's beds and stroked them or fed them. You got some recognition sometimes, but not a lot other times, because they're on their last legs. So when the sister asked me how I'd got on I said, 'I was there.' And she said to me, 'What was St. John or Our Blessed Mother doing at the foot of the Cross?' "

Do we look at the poor with compassion? They are hungry not only for food, they are hungry to be recognized as human beings. They are hungry for dignity and to be treated as we are treated. They are hungry for our love.

EVERY

ACT

OF

LOVE

IS

A

PRAYER

❧

It is not how much you do but how much love you put into the doing and sharing with others that is important. Try not to judge people. If you judge others then you are not giving love. Instead, try to help them by seeing their needs and acting to meet them. People often ask me what I think about homosexuals, for example, and I always answer that I don't judge people. It isn't what anyone may or may not have done, but what *you* have done that matters in God's eyes.

We have the following words in a sign outside our chapel at the Mother House. They were written by Father Edward Le Joly after we had talked in 1977, and explain exactly what our work is about:

We are not here for the work, we are here for Jesus. All we do is for Him. We are first of all religious, we are not social workers, not teachers, not nurses or doctors, we are religious sisters. We serve Jesus in the poor. We nurse Him, feed Him, clothe Him, visit Him, comfort Him in the poor, the abandoned, the sick, the orphans, the dying. But all we do, our prayer, our work, our suffering is for Jesus. Our life has no other reason or motivation. This is a point many people do not understand.*

Here are some words and examples from Sister Dolores, Brother Geoff, and a volunteer, Linda, on this kind of love in action:

"In the West there is so much loneliness. Most lonely people just need someone to sit with them, be with them, smile at them, because many do not have any family left and are living alone, are shut in. So on different occasions during the year, when I was working in one of our homes in New York, we would bring these people all together for a social gathering so that they could meet others, and they really looked forward to that. We'd organize a special day for them—we'd give them a good lunch and some cakes—and just by having them come out of their homes and mix with others we brought happiness into their lives.

"In our soup kitchens we provide for people who are drifters. They come for a meal, and some of them

* Edward Le Joly. *We Do It for Jesus: Mother Teresa and Her Missionaries of Charity* (Queens Village, NY: Oxford University Press, 1977).

don't eat at all. They just want to be there in an atmo-sphere of peace and tranquillity and usually after we share a prayer or something, they leave. Most people don't just want soup, they want contact where they are appreciated, loved, feel wanted, and find some peace in their hearts. It's the personal touch that matters."

"In the West we have a tendency to be profit-oriented, where everything is measured according to the results and we get caught up in being more and more active to generate results. In the East—especially in India—I find that people are more content to just *be*, to just sit around under a banyan tree for half a day chatting to each other. We Westerners would probably call that wasting time. But there is value to it. Being with someone, listening without a clock and without anticipation of results, teaches us about love. The suc-cess of love is in the loving—it is not in the result of loving. Of course it is natural in love to want the best for the other person, but whether it turns out that way or not does not determine the value of what we have done. The more we can remove this priority for results the more we can learn about the contemplative ele-ment of love. There is the love expressed in the service and the love in the contemplation. It is the balance of both which we should be striving for. Love is the key to finding this balance."

"Helping the children at Shishu Bhavan in Cal-cutta was very special for me. I felt very moved by them. One morning we sat upstairs in a circle—we'd do that a lot and sit and sing—and I was holding a little handicapped boy who just looked at me with complete joy and love in his eyes. He had a very deep serenity in him. I remember this as a deeply spiritual experience."

LOVING
UNTIL
IT
HURTS

We must grow in love and to do this we must go on loving and loving and giving and giving until it hurts—the way Jesus did. Do ordinary things with extraordinary love: little things like caring for the sick and the homeless, the lonely and the unwanted, washing and cleaning for them.

You must give what will cost you something. This, then, is giving not just what you can live without but what you can't live without or don't want to live without, something you really like. Then your gift becomes a sacrifice, which will have value before God. Any sacrifice is useful if it is done out of love.

This giving until it hurts—this sacrifice—is also what I call love in action. Every day I see this love—in children, men, and women. I was once walking down the street and a beggar came to me and he said,

"Mother Teresa, everybody's giving to you, I also want to give to you. Today, for the whole day, I got only twenty-nine paise and I want to give it to you." I thought for a moment: If I take it he will have nothing to eat tonight, and if I don't take it I will hurt him. So I put out my hands and I took the money. I have never seen such joy on anybody's face as I saw on his—that a beggar, he too, could give to Mother Teresa. It was a big sacrifice for that poor man who'd been sitting in the sun all day and had only received twenty-nine paise. It was beautiful: twenty-nine paise is such a small amount and I can get nothing with it, but as he gave it up and I took it, it became like thousands because it was given with so much love.

The other day I received a letter from a small child in America. I knew he was little because he wrote in big handwriting, "Mother Teresa I love you so much I'm sending you my pocket money," and inside the letter there was a check for three dollars. Also, one of the sisters in London told me that, one day, a little girl came to the door of the home in Kilburn with a bag of pennies and she said, "This is for the poor men." She didn't say, "This is for Mother Teresa" or "for the Missionaries of Charity." She lived down the road and had seen all the residents walking around—and so she said, "This is for the men." She'd just seen with her eyes and I think it's like that for so many people. They see something and they're attracted towards it because it's good.

A young couple got married here recently. They

decided to keep their wedding simple—she wore a plain cotton sari and there were just his and her parents' present—and they gave us all the money they had saved from not having a big Hindu wedding ceremony. They were sharing their love with the poor. Something like this happens every day. By becoming poor ourselves, by loving until it hurts, we become capable of loving more deeply, more beautifully, more wholly.

One of our volunteers, Sarah, gives her experiences of this kind of love while working in one of our homes in San Francisco:

"What I perceive as loving until it hurts is loving even if you don't understand the situation, the people, anything. It's easier said than done, but there are periods of time when I can do it. The result of getting close to people, on the other hand, is that when one of the residents—Chris—died it was really hard for me. I didn't want to go back—in fact I didn't for two or three weeks. I'd get up in the morning and get ready—and then I didn't go. The sisters understood this so well. That's how they helped me, because there's no judgment or condemnation from them. They said, 'That's fine—come back whenever you want.' When I mourned and cried for Chris after he died, I was told, 'This house is here for men to die. It would be selfish for us to cry because we're then thinking of ourselves and not thinking about where they are—with God. We should be happy for them.' That's their attitude.

"I'm not even a full-time volunteer and the people who do that work at the house day by day must know much more about this loving until it hurts. If you are in that environment and give all the time, you're going to become more fine-tuned in the art of loving and become a spiritual resource for God. These full-time volunteers are special—God fills them up every day. It's so much easier to fake love in the world because nobody really demands that you give until it hurts—until they are sick."

A
CHEERFUL
SUFFERER

❧

The spirit of a Missionary of Charity is total surrender to God, loving trust in others, and cheerfulness with everyone. We have to accept suffering with joy, we have to live a life of poverty with cheerful trust and to minister to Jesus in the poorest of the poor with cheerfulness. God loves a cheerful giver. She or he gives best who gives with a smile. If you are always ready to say Yes to God, you will naturally have a smile for all and be able, with God's blessing, to give until it hurts.

Two of our volunteers, Sarah and Dave, discovered the value of this approach in our homes in San Francisco and London:

"What I really like about the sisters is that when things get difficult they keep a sense of humor about it. And, when mistakes are made, they're rectified and then we go on. But again, some of them have told me that their lives are sometimes very hard and they are sorrowful and they do cry for their own families. You know they have brothers, sisters, parents who have problems or are sick and they can't do anything to help them in this world except to pray. So they have feelings, they cry too. They are human—they love God and they love people."

"I found out from working with the sisters that they are just who they appear to be. I have a lot of daily contact with them, doing the ordinary things we do, like working in the kitchen and scrubbing the floors, serving meals, driving to the supermarket and then taking people to the doctor or to a psychiatric unit in the hospital, and dealing sometimes with some very unpleasant people on the way. And they are always so cheerful. It's not that gritted-teeth cheerfulness, it's the real thing.

"I'm convinced that the external cheerfulness is the manifestation of an inward joy that they feel. I know that anyone who works with them is aware of the time they spend in the chapel on their knees, and they are very happy because of it. Their happiest time is when they pray—they look forward to it, they are eager to pray and to refuel and they are equally eager to come out of that refueling and give away the energy that they receive. This is not a fanaticism, it is a genuine joyful desire to share what they have. Just as they don't keep any of the material things that they have: anything that's given to them, clothing or food or money or whatever it may be—paper bags, rubber bands, you name it—they give it away. Everything that comes in goes out.

"I think how much God gives them and how much He must love them. I love them, and I am drawn to them by how pleasing they must be to God. Their grace and their energy are given to them by Him—it's reciprocal love, which they then show to us. I see this in every single one of the sisters, and yet they are not clones, they are their own individual selves, they have their own personalities."

The password of the early Christians was joy, so let us still serve the Lord with joy. Sister Kateri explains how this feels:

"I was working at the cerebral palsy center in New York and I was praying daily. One day somebody asked me what I was so happy about, intimating that I might have fallen in love with someone. But it wasn't exactly that—it was just feeling the love of God. I was so happy and so fulfilled as my relationship with God was growing. This made me full of joy."

Joy is love, joy is prayer, joy is strength. God loves a person who gives joyfully, and if you give joyfully you always give more. A joyful heart is the result of a heart burning with love.

Works of love are always works of joy. We don't need to look for happiness: if we have love for others we'll be given it. It is the gift of God.

SERVICE

THE
FRUIT
OF
LOVE
IS
SERVICE

We have a sign on the wall of the children's home in Calcutta that reads:

TAKE TIME TO THINK
TAKE TIME TO PRAY
TAKE TIME TO LAUGH

IT IS THE SOURCE OF POWER
IT IS THE GREATEST POWER ON EARTH
IT IS THE MUSIC OF THE SOUL

TAKE TIME TO PLAY
TAKE TIME TO LOVE AND BE LOVED
TAKE TIME TO GIVE

IT IS THE SECRET OF PERPETUAL YOUTH
IT IS GOD'S GIVEN PRIVILEGE
IT IS TOO SHORT A DAY TO BE SELFISH

TAKE TIME TO READ
TAKE TIME TO BE FRIENDLY
TAKE TIME TO WORK

IT IS THE FOUNTAIN OF WISDOM
IT IS THE ROAD TO HAPPINESS
IT IS THE PRICE OF SUCCESS

TAKE TIME TO DO CHARITY
IT IS THE KEY TO HEAVEN.

Prayer in action is love, and love in action is service. Try to give unconditionally whatever a person needs in the moment. The point is to do *something*, however small, and show you care through your actions by giving your time. Sometimes this may mean doing something physical (such as we do in our homes for the sick and dying) or sometimes it may mean offering spiritual support for the shut-ins (those isolated and lonely in their own homes). If an ill person wants medicine, then give him medicine; if he needs comfort, then comfort him.

We are all God's children so it is important to share His gifts. Do not worry about why problems exist in the world—just respond to people's needs. Some say to me that if we give charity to others it'll diminish the responsibility of government towards the needy and the poor. I don't concern myself with this, because governments do not usually offer love. I just do what I can do: the rest is not my business.

God has been so good to us: works of love are always a means of becoming closer to God. Look at what Jesus did in His life on earth! He spent it just doing good. I remind the sisters that three years of Jesus's life were spent healing the sick and the lepers, children and other people; and that's exactly what we're doing, preaching the Gospel through our actions. It is a privilege for us to serve, and it's a real, wholehearted service that we try and give.

We feel what we are doing is just a drop in the ocean, but that ocean would be less without that drop. For instance, we started our schools to teach poor children to love learning and to be clean. If we hadn't, these children would be left on the streets.

If someone can be better cared for by another organization, depending on the circumstances, then we advise it, but because we are serving the poorest of the poor we never turn a person away if they show real need.

Brother Geoff explains it in this way:

"Very rarely can we find someone who will take care of our abandoned people, especially in countries like India where the needs are enormous. Our Missionaries of Charity homes are often the last stop for many patients who are already rejected by just about everyone else."

In order to show more of the fruits of love in action, I thought it would be helpful first of all to offer a flavor of the work of the Missionaries of Charity, and then to share experiences of some of those who have volunteered to help us. In this way you will see the effect that doing something, however small, can have—not only on the deprived, but also on the person doing the caring.

Today, the work of the Missionaries of Charity is very varied and can be divided into the following:

APOSTOLIC WORK through Sunday schools, Bible study groups, Catholic action groups, and the visiting of those in hospitals, nursing homes, and prisons.

MEDICAL CARE through dispensaries, leprosy clinics, rehabilitation centers for leprosy patients. Also through our homes for abandoned children, physically and mentally disabled children, sick and dying destitutes, AIDS patients, and TB patients, and our malnutrition centers and mobile clinics.

EDUCATIONAL SERVICE through primary schools in the slums, sewing classes, commercial classes, handicraft classes, village preschools, and after-school programs.

SOCIAL SERVICE through child welfare and education

schemes; day crèches; homes for the homeless, alcoholics, and drug addicts; homes for unmarried
mothers; night shelters; and natural family planning centers.

RELIEF SERVICE through food and clothing centers,
where we provide dry rations, cooked meals, and
family emergency relief.

GANDHIJI PREM NIVAS, TITAGARH, CALCUTTA

Today, leprosy patients can have a life, knowing that
they can get help and be cured. It is no longer necessary to disappear and hide if one has leprosy, and this
means the whole family can now live together without
fear of infection. A child born of a leper is now not a
leper.

More than forty years ago we decided to start a
mobile clinic for leprosy patients under a tree at
Titagarh, several kilometers outside Calcutta. We saw
patients twice a week and on the other days took care
of those suffering from malnutrition and visited the
homes of the sick. Then, on Saturdays, we'd do their
cleaning.

Today, we have a wonderful center called Gandhiji Prem Nivas, which is almost a village in itself.
Spread alongside the railway line, the buildings are
painted in bright, cheerful colors: reds and blues and
greens. There are workshops, dormitories, clinics,

wards, a school, an outpatients' department, and also individual huts for families—as well as pools that provide the whole community with its water. Just inside the inner courtyard is a statue of Gandhi.

Prem Nivas was built by the leprosy patients themselves and is a place where they can both live and work. When we first were given the land to develop a center in 1974, it was a railway dump yard. We began by building simple thatched huts and slowly it turned into something quite beautiful.

Brother Vinod, who runs Prem Nivas, gives more information on the place today:

"We have 1,400 leprosy cases under regular treatment per month and 38,000 have registered here since 1958. Many of them have been released from treatment; but those people we are now looking after are going to live for another twenty to thirty years, so the Missionaries of Charity will at least continue this work for that length of time. Now that leprosy can be controlled I am sure we will not see as much deformity in the future—the government's plan is to eradicate leprosy in India by the year 2000.

"Early detection is the key, and this is why our clinic is so vital. The disease affects the body's immune system and is an airborne one—so you don't have to be in touch with a patient for a long period to catch it. If your immune system is strong, however, you will not be affected. We do not have a vaccination against the disease but we do have a test which determines one's immunity. And if anyone does catch it, it can be cured with drugs at an early stage.

"Leprosy is still found mostly among the poorer sections of society. The poor don't have the education to know what they are suffering from until the deformity sets in. Then, of course, it's too late to alter the damage when there is loss of sensation in the hands and feet and ulceration, though we can halt further spread at this point. However, leprosy patients with visible deformities become desperate and don't want to live in a society which rejects them. So we offer a place here, and a job, and within a short time a patient's faith and hope and self-esteem return.

"We admit many beggars who have previously lived on the footpath or at the railway station. We also take in small children with leprosy. Their parents always say that the moment their child is better, they'll return to take him or her back—but they never do. So this is the home for the boys and girls as well, and when they grow up they usually marry here, get a job, their own house, and stay with us.

"All the work is done by the patients—they train others in dressing, injections, and ward maintenance. They take care of their own brethren. They understand the sufferings and difficulties of other patients so much better than we do. Of course the brothers are trained in leprosy care. They are paramedical workers and treat patients along with the doctors, who perform surgery once a week and offer their time for nothing. But the patient-to-patient contact is always preferable.

"We are very self-sufficient—we grow our own vegetables and whenever we have a surplus we offer it to the other homes. We have fish in the fishery and goats and other animals on our small farm, as well as a handloom section [in which the sisters' saris are made], cobblers and carpenters, builders and engineers. There's regular work for everyone."

SHISHU BHAVAN, CALCUTTA

Shishu Bhavan, our children's home in Calcutta, is made up of a number of tall buildings behind a wall on a busy main road. At the entrance are the day clinics, where the poor can bring their children, and the adoption offices. In rooms inside are the infants and small babies, in row upon row of green cots. There is also a small courtyard for the children to run around in as well as a room where they can play games and have their meals.

Shishu Bhavan is run by Sister Charmaine Jose. She and her sisters look after about 300 sick or malnourished children at any one time, as well as poor unmarried mothers, whom they provide with jobs.

There is also an outpatient section at which three doctors dispense medical attention to perhaps 1,000 to

2,000 patients a week. Then there is the adoption parlor for those who want to discuss adopting some of the children. When children reach the age of ten and are not adopted, we sometimes send them to boarding schools to be educated and then to college, or to a secretarial course, and we get them work. Once they have settled into their own lives, we usually help them get married and give them a dowry to start them off. They are very happy about this and they bring their own children back regularly to visit. I often tell them they are lucky in having not just one mother-in-law but twenty!

On the ground floor of Shishu Bhavan there are cooking facilities to feed over 1,000 people daily. These are usually beggars from the street and this is the one place they can rely on for one meal a day, which is all they get. However, there are also unforeseen disasters that occur, and then we need to be in attendance and offer relief services. For instance, when a large area near Calcutta was flooded and washed away, 1,200 families were left stranded with nothing. Sisters from Shishu Bhavan, and also brothers, worked all night taking them supplies and offering shelter.

As Sister Charmaine Jose describes:

"We are street people and our work is in the streets. We pray as we walk, going out to visit families, to be with a dying child, or to bring medicine to those in need. Each sister takes one street a day to see what help we can give the poor. We also go out to the villages where there are hardly any facilities and we open medical centers there. Sometimes we take care of 2,500 patients a week in these places.

"Many of our sisters are trained nurses and some are doctors, so they usually work in the dispensaries, though the ones trained to take care of children work in the wards. We also have a school for street children who are abused and in prostitution. They are usually without food, support, or medicine. So we collect them up, teach them, feed them, dress them, and then after a while find a sponsor to support each individual, to enable them to go to a real school and complete their education.

"The mentally and physically disabled children remain in our care here. A lot of them don't live long but the ones who do we transfer to our other homes when they reach the age of thirteen."

NIRMAL HRIDAY, CALCUTTA

Our home for the dying in Calcutta was once a place for pilgrims to rest after traveling to the Kali temple. Deep in the busy heart of the Kalighat area of the city, our building is actually joined to the temple itself. On the left side as you enter, we have the men's ward, and on the right the women's. Tall, thin windows bring beams of light into the rooms, which are full of row upon row of beds, all covered by blue plastic mattress covers. In between the wards are the medical center and the baths, and behind them are the kitchen and the morgue. Our school for street children is on the roof, where the sisters live.

We have 50 beds for men and 55 for women, but we can increase this number according to need. When men and women first come to the home for the dying, they are not usually able to speak for themselves, so when they arrive in ambulances or the sisters or brothers bring them in, they are placed in the register as "unknown." Then, with a little care and love and some food, they do manage to speak and give their names. The sisters try and find out what religion they are, too—so that when they die they can have the appropriate burial. The Catholics go to the cemetery, the Muslims to the Muslim burial place, and the Hindus to the burning ghat, which is very close to us. The majority of people who come to us are Hindus, so if we don't know their religion, we usually give them a Hindu burial.

Sister Dolores, who runs Nirmal Hriday, says:

"We never ask people why they are on the street: we don't need to know their history. We don't judge them for whatever situation they are in, because all they want is some love and care and they are satisfied.

We just look after the person who is brought to us and God does the rest through us.

"What usually happens when a person arrives is that she or he is given a bath. But sometimes a person is so ill that we just give her a bed, wash her face, and put her on an IV drip. Sometimes we need to care for those with gangrene or bad wounds with maggots or chronic diarrhea. Many arrive with TB and some are bleeding—the bleeding must be stopped first of all.

"Sometimes, as soon as a patient lies on the bed she dies. At other times, patients get a little better, can sit up in bed or stand or walk about, and some of them go back home, although home for many is just the street. So some leave us and then return if they get sick again. We say we will keep a bed for them."

THE BRITISH ISLES

Sister Theresina is the American-born Regional Superior for the British Isles and Ireland. Here, she describes our growing work in Britain:

"When the sisters started working here we found we were needed to help a lot of pensioner shut-ins. We'd often find an old couple with no heater in the middle of winter and so we'd provide one, or we'd find people living without furniture for one reason or another. Some people are very simple and they don't know whom to contact—behind brick walls there are a lot of lonely people very much in need of a visit.

"In the early days, we used to go out at night to look for the homeless. Today, we have a men's and women's shelter in Kilburn in London; and in Liverpool, in the north of England, we have a men's home, a women's home, and a soup kitchen—and we also do pastoral work, family visiting, and catechism programs for children there. Sometimes we take people for outings and organize special occasions for them—for instance, we took 320 people in six coaches on a trip to Worth Abbey recently.

"We pray the Rosary as we go out—it's our weapon, the word of God. The devil tries to influence people's lives, and we have to try and penetrate that and go with Jesus and with Mary, because they are the ones who have to work and touch people's hearts—not us. We are very much attached to the Rosary. I remember when we prayed it once on the Underground train in London. We kept our voices low because people don't talk very much in England on public transport, and it was quiet in the carriage. Then the train had a fault so we all had to get out and wait on the platform and the next train that came was quite overcrowded. A lady was standing next to us and said, 'Sister, I want you to know that I have been sharing the Rosary with you, have been praying along with you,' and we were unaware that she had been doing so. She said that sometimes she comes to our house in Bravington Road to the holy hour but hadn't come for a while. And that was our conversation, but it helped us because we don't always see the fruits of what we are doing.

"When Mother came to the men's home in Kilburn in March 1994 she saw two rooms and said, 'These are for the AIDS patients.' This was the first time I'd heard about us possibly taking AIDS patients but Mother just said it—she was inspired, I think, because I remember how she looked while standing in the room and saying it. So I tried to make it a reality and it wasn't easy. Now, through the help of a man who is a recovered alcoholic and drug addict, and who has AIDS himself, we are receiving people who cannot fend for themselves."

THE WORK OF THE BROTHERS

Brother Geoff is Australian and succeeded the founding General Servant, Brother Andrew, as head of the Missionaries of Charity Brothers.

"In Los Angeles our main work is a day center for Latino illegal immigrants, many of whom are living on the street. This is a place where, three days a week, 75 to 100 young people aged fourteen to eighteen come in for a hot meal, a shower, medical treatment, a haircut—and to relax. In the men's unit, we care for 8 men who are physically and mentally handicapped.

These men have also been found on the streets of Los Angeles and are desperately in need of attention and a secure environment.

"In Japan, in Tokyo, we work with alcoholic men from the street. This is full-time work. Occasionally there have been fights and things can get rough sometimes—we try to keep violence out of our homes. The Japanese alcoholics are usually fairly well behaved compared to those in other countries. In Los Angeles we have had brothers working with gang boys to help them, and in Hong Kong we had someone working with drug addicts. We also work in tougher areas—in cities like Bogotá and Medellín in Colombia, where there is a lot of violence around. We witness a lot but keep ourselves uninvolved. People know the work we are doing and usually don't disturb us.

"Our work differs a lot from other organizations' work with the poor. That is not to say that one is better than the other—I think good is done on both sides—but many efforts are made by others to take the poor man and help him step beyond his station, beyond the situation that made him poor in the first place. This is a worthwhile effort, especially through education, but it can become a political issue. The poor the Missionaries of Charity feel called to work with are those who, no matter what you do for them, are still going to be dependent in some way on others. We are constantly asked, 'Instead of giving a man a fish, why don't you teach him to fish?' and we answer that most of our poor people wouldn't have the strength to even hold a fishing rod. And I often think that this is where there is confusion—and sometimes criticism—about our work, because no distinction is made between our kind of poor and other kinds of poor.

"Development is certainly worthwhile but development is not what our poor people need. If a man is dying, there is no time to go into why he is in this condition and list all the social programs which could have prevented it. What we are saying is, 'Let others work on the problems that have put this man in this condition, but let us help him to die in peace and dignity now.' In many cases, we offer more short-term care than they do and simply say: This man or woman is in need—what can we do to help them? If political changes will alleviate this situation in the future then we welcome them, but we don't have the time or energy, or often the ability, to do much about it. God, in His wisdom, puts it all together. He knows that no one person can cover the whole situation so he inspires certain people to work in certain areas and others to work in others."

THERE

IS

SO

MUCH

WORK

TO

DO

❧

We have so many requests for opening new homes around the world and we are doing this all the time. We are now in well over a hundred countries—this is a real gift of God, to be able to give wholehearted free service to the poorest of the poor in so many places. For example, we have AIDS homes now in Spain, in Portugal, in Brazil, and in Honduras. In Africa we do the work but do not have specific homes in themselves, and the same is true in Haiti. In the United States we also have AIDS homes—in New York; Washington, D.C.; Baltimore; Dallas; Atlanta; San Francisco; and elsewhere. We are now opening our first home for AIDS patients in India, in Bombay. We have also just started an orphanage in Washington and we have been hoping to open a home in China for quite a while.

There is always more work to do, but the following ex-
amples from Sister Dolores show how joyful opening a new
home can be:

"In 1965 we were asked by the Bishop of
Cocorote to open a home in Venezuela. It was a real
joy for me to be part of the first house that Mother
opened outside India. She wanted only to send professed sisters, not junior professed, of which I was one;
but she used to ask us if there were any volunteers and
we would all put our hands up. I was in Delhi at the
time helping another sister at the children's home there
and I had a chance to be with Mother. She pulled me
aside and said, 'Jesus wants you to go to Venezuela.'

"I was so happy that it was God's plan for me to
go, and so it was that a group of us arrived on July 26,
1965. Now they offer a Mass of Thanksgiving for
the arrival of the sisters every year on that day and
they also prepare a special feast for the poor people in
that home.

"When we arrived we had no idea of the language or customs of the people. It was completely different, but again that was the challenge God gave us.
Everyone received us joyfully and taught us a few
words, and when we'd learned them they then helped
us by completing our sentences since we hadn't the
time to sit down and study. Cocorote was a beautiful
mission for me and the people there are very dear to
my heart, even now after all these years.

"In 1985, it was Cardinal O'Connor who helped

us open our first home for AIDS patients in New York. The need had originally come from the Sing Sing prison and we received our first patients from there. They had usually been taken first to St. Clare's Hospital or Bellevue or Mount Sinai. We'd visit them, and then, if it was appropriate for them to come to us, they would. They were usually the ones who were rejected or who had nobody and carried a lot of bitterness in their hearts. Coping with the last stages of life is hard, so we'd take time to create a family spirit among them—we'd eat together, talk, pray, and play together. Many were not close to their families, but after being with us for a while, and through the gift of God, they'd be brought together with their parents. Some would write letters and others would telephone. And, as we grew, one sick man would take care of another—which was always wonderful to witness."

THE
CATCHING
FORCE—
ACTING
THE
SIMPLE
WAY

O ur work is constant, our homes are full. The problems of the poor continue, so our work continues. Yet everyone, not just the Missionaries of Charity, can do something beautiful for God by reaching out to the poor people in their own countries. I see no lack of hesitation in helping others. I see only people filled with God's love, wanting to do works of love. This is the future—this is God's wish for us—to serve through love in action, and to be inspired by the Holy Spirit to act when called.

We would not be able to do our work without our volunteers. They come from many different backgrounds, cultures, and faiths. All that we require of them is to be able to give love and time to others. We welcome them with these words, which we have as a poster in the Mother House:

YOU HAVE COME TO SERVE CHRIST IN THE CRIPPLED, THE
    SICK AND THE DYING.

WE ARE HAPPY AND THANKFUL THAT YOU HAVE TAKEN
    THIS OPPORTUNITY TO BE A WITNESS OF GOD'S
    LOVE IN ACTION.

REMEMBER THAT IT IS CHRIST WHO WORKS THROUGH
    US—WE ARE MERELY INSTRUMENTS FOR SERVICE.

IT IS NOT HOW MUCH WE DO, BUT HOW MUCH LOVE
    WE PUT INTO THE DOING.

*Sister Dolores has much experience in working with the
volunteers, and she offers this advice:*

"Volunteers who come and work with us must
have an open mind and be available for any work, because that is how God wants everyone to be. Most
work alongside the sisters and the brothers in the spirit
of Mother Teresa and the Missionaries of Charity because our way is completely different from that of the
world outside or other charitable institutions. Our way
is simple and those who come to help and share in the
work must do it along with us. For instance, if I say,
'Go and take this patient to the hospital' or 'Just give
her a bath now,' the helper must be open to doing it
because we don't follow a set of rules. The men and
women who come, though, work very hard."

Sister Theresina in London agrees:

"Volunteers are a big help to us and we rely on them to a certain extent, although we have to be ready to do everything ourselves. If we need volunteer help we pray for it and if it doesn't come we ask the poor to help us, and they are very happy to do so. We always manage in our simple way—we cook up a meal and serve it. The thing is to continually offer this service, offer this help, and if volunteers come it just makes us more efficient."

Here is a comment from one of our volunteers about what you can both give and receive from helping out. Mary is a doctor who worked with us at Kalighat for a while:

"Imagine going into a place and being told: 'Go and bathe that one.' It's an incredible privilege that you don't have to say who you are, all you have to have is a willingness to help—and you're judged on that. That is one of the things about Mother's work—to let people come in contact with the poor. It's as much for our sake as for theirs. We've crossed this enormous divide, you know, it's not just these 'millions' of people, but somebody you've actually touched."

LOVE
IN
ACTION

I n this section some of our volunteers around the
world, laymen and -women, share their experiences
of what it feels like to serve the poor and how they have
found they can do something in their own communities.

The volunteers who come to Calcutta help mostly with the
sick and the dying, or they help with our children at
Shishu Bhavan. They are beautiful people who give so
generously. Many make great sacrifices to come here, to
share in the work of loving the poor, feeling the closeness
of Jesus. Being here, for some, gives them the chance to
really deepen their personal love for Him:

DONNA

"I'm a nurse by training and I took a break from
Scotland, where I live, to do some traveling. I was

working in Sydney when the idea of helping Mother Teresa's missionaries just popped into my head. I'm not a Catholic—I was brought up Scottish Presbyterian and my father is an atheist. I think my decision to go to India came after I had seen the movie *Gandhi*. I was not so much interested in Indian history as I was in Gandhi's philosophy and the kind of selfless and humble life he expressed. It intrigued me to see the connection between his philosophy and that of Mother Teresa.

"After writing to Calcutta and being invited to come along, I started to work at the children's home, Shishu Bhavan. My first impression of the Mother House and the other homes was their simplicity and their peace. They were like havens amid all the noise and the filth I experienced on the streets of Calcutta.

"Since working with the Missionaries of Charity I would say that a number of things have changed in my life—you can't stay there for any length of time without some major shift in your life taking place. I am not shocked anymore about seeing poverty and dirt, and am now more practical in what I feel I can do for poor people. I know that when I return home I will probably get involved in working with the homeless. And being around the sisters with their never-ending faith has comforted me, helped me in doing this work—their joy and faith is infectious, you know. It seems that whoever comes here and works as a volunteer gets the message and takes it away to put it into action at home. Do *something*, that's the point of it, and we don't have to come continually to Calcutta and try to be like the sisters to do so."

LINDA

"I did very much feel as if it wasn't me that wanted to go to Calcutta. It was almost like I was being pushed there. Certainly, I just knew that going to Calcutta was the right thing to do, that it was a calling. Many people who go to volunteer in India think they are doing it consciously, but in fact they are doing it on another, deeper level. From the volunteers I got to know, I'd say they all had this internal voice that came to them—it just hit them that this was what they had to do. At first, I was very nervous about the poverty, noise, and squalor of India and I went around in a daze for about a day or so until I got used to it. Then I started to work at Shishu Bhavan, the children's home. I'd work there in the mornings and then be free in the afternoons.

"For the first couple of days I was completely ecstatic—I thought, 'I'm so wonderful, I'm doing all these wonderful things looking after these children, I'm giving them loads of love and they just smile at me and love me.' I felt so brilliant and so holy! And then, after three days, I had a complete breakdown because I suddenly realized that I was a terrible person to be going there for only a short while. I was playing with these children, cuddling them, giving them lots of attention—and at the end of my time there I was coming back to my nice cozy little place in England, my nice cushy job, and my weekly wage. I was giving sweets to a baby and then taking them away again. I started to cry, I had felt so good, such a good person, and now I realized that I wasn't, because I was volunteering for me, not them. I was giving because of something in me that needed healing, and that was the need I had for love.

"A volunteer who had been there much longer than I comforted me and said, 'Whatever love you give, however small, they wouldn't have had if you hadn't come, or given it. Each volunteer who will come after you will give them a little more.' It made me appreciate the sisters even more. In their devotional life they have no thought for themselves. They really are in the hands of God and it's beautiful. It is so rare to see anybody as completely devoted to something like that. That affected me for life. And, as the Gospel says, I received much more than I gave. I left Calcutta with a sense that it was a very special place, that God was working there, that a good force was operating there."

JUDITH

"I was working with the poor in Melbourne, Australia, in a home for homeless alcoholic men and I did this throughout my university years. I really enjoyed it and realized that I wanted to try and do something in welfare in another country. This stayed at the back of my mind until, for various reasons, the time was right to leave Australia. I came to Calcutta because I knew about the Loreto order of nuns, as I had been educated by them in Australia. I was intending to teach English first of all, but I came in contact with the volunteer community here and became a full-time volunteer with the Missionaries of Charity. I've been here six months now and like the way we work. I go to Kalighat, to the home for the dying, and every morning at eight o'clock Sister Dolores begins our work with reflection. We each speak with her for five or ten minutes about our experiences, our thoughts, to share our stories. It is entirely optional and not meant to be specifically religious—there are all sorts of people who come with totally differing views—but to have this time is essential before we go into action.

"You really do have to leave behind what you are trained to do because this is not a hospital, it's a home. The care may be basic, but it's not careless. There's a lot to experience, and sometimes I felt quite fragile and emotional about the suffering. It totally saturated me after a few months here, so much so that I couldn't handle simple things like taking care of a woman with bedsores. I wasn't able to dress a wound because I was running on emotional empty. I took three weeks' holiday—the sisters are completely nonjudgmental and encourage us to take time off, to look after ourselves, because they know how hard the work can be. When I returned from my break I worked for three months straight, these three months being the best time I have had here. I have a sense of satisfaction in allowing myself to experience this suffering. Kalighat is extraordinary because we live with life and death every day.

"Since I've been here I have renewed my Catholic faith. As far as the spiritual Christian experience that I am having here goes, I feel very much alive. It is not now a matter of belief, it's just knowing that there is something inside myself that's breathing. And being surrounded by death all day I am awed by the dignity of the service to women [female volunteers work with the women] who come here to be clothed, fed, and treated like human beings after they've been living their lives like animals. The significant part for me is that these women die with someone there, people around them who actually really care for them, see that they are clean, and so on. The dignity of death is extraordinary—this is the important thing about Kalighat.

"I know that I will continue to work with the poor because of the satisfaction and the happiness it brings to me. I've been happier here than I've ever been, so I shouldn't ignore this. There's something in it, something there. In hindsight I see how unhappy I was in the past—a lot of people I know have this feeling, this restlessness, and convince themselves they are content."

MICHAEL

"My wife Jane and I started an association called TRACKS (Training Resources and Care for Kids) two years ago after seeing the need of the children who live on the platform of Howrah Station in Calcutta, and who don't get very much care. The Missionary of Charity brothers come here in the mornings, do their rounds, and provide some medical care, but we could see they were unable to service all the problems. For instance, we'd sometimes find babies born on the platform or abandoned, or the bigger boys sexually exploiting the younger boys and girls—and there was no protection for these young children.

"We had nothing when we started but when we asked Mother Teresa for some supplies she gave us medicines to get us going. Now, if any of our children are very ill and need constant care, the sisters of Shishu Bhavan will accept them. We've been arrested a couple of times by the authorities; but once Mother Teresa had written a letter to the station management on our behalf, we found we had few further problems from them.

"Our work is to look after, on an average day, 35 to 40 children between the ages of one and sixteen. We supply a full-time doctor and nurse and two teachers, and we have a games master and medical officer and three volunteers from various other countries. We teach the children in a school—the basic subjects covered are mathematics and geography and how to live in normal social conditions, because this is a non-formal education and we can train children to go on to regular schools from here. We provide all our education in three languages: Hindi, Bengali, and English."

PENNY

"Like so many volunteers I got to know, I landed up in Calcutta 'by accident.' I was literally just stopping over on my way to Australia. I was a beauty therapist at the time; I'd recently been divorced and an old friend had bought me a ticket to see her. I turned up at the YWCA and was immediately welcomed by this volunteer coordinator for the Missionaries of Charity. She said, 'I've been praying for someone and you arrived.' She asked me if I could help her go into the slums and invite children to take part in a Christmas play at the Mother House. There I was in my tight little skirt and high heels, can you imagine?

"A few days later I went to Kalighat for the first time. It was terribly traumatic for me—being a beauty therapist I was used to everything being all nice and spick-and-span, smelling nice, so it was quite a shock. When one of the sisters asked me to wash this woman I just thought, There's no way. I just couldn't. I just stood there. She called me over and said, 'Penny, please. Take her.' I just cried and said I couldn't. So she said, 'All right, come with me,' and she picked up this little bundle of bones, because that's what this lady was, and took her into the bathroom. Even now it makes me cry—there wasn't a lot of light in the room and I was still absolutely catatonic. Then all of a sudden the whole room just lit up! One minute I was saying 'I can't' and the next I realized, of course, I could.

"It suddenly struck me, seeing one of those religious pictures they have on the wall—it was the body of Christ—that anybody can be Christ. It wasn't just that little old lady covered in scabies, it was the whole world that was the body of Christ. I realized that what I was doing for one I could do for anybody.

"I stayed for six months, and when I was leaving Calcutta, I said to Mother Teresa, 'I'll come back.' She answered, 'You won't come back—there's a lot to do where you live. Things will happen, God will tell you what to do.' I had always been frustrated because I couldn't help my clients with the psychological problems that surfaced when I was giving them beauty treatments. I had found that as soon as a woman took her clothes off in the cubicle, she became the child, she became the person who had so much to release. We would start chatting and she would come out with all these problems that I didn't know how to deal with. I could help her relax but I couldn't help whatever it was deep inside that was hurting. I realized that I could train to be a psychotherapist as well—and I did.

"Now when old people tell me they're stuck and too old to change I say, 'I'm sorry but I disagree and I've got experience of it—at forty-eight I changed my life completely.'"

The previous pages have told some of the experiences of the people who have helped us in Calcutta. But I say again that you don't have to come to India to give love to others—the street you live on can be your Nirmal Hriday. You can help the poor in your own country, as the following stories show:

DAVE

"I started volunteering with the Missionaries of Charity in early 1994 after sitting in front of the television and watching the horrors in Rwanda and Somalia. My wife was away on a business trip so I was on my own and didn't have anything that I had to do. I started thinking as I was watching the news, God, there's got to be a lot of work to do and so many places and so much needed, somebody ought to get over there and do something about it. And then I found myself thinking, Here you sit, put up or shut up. So I said at that time that I'd see if there were any organizations that could use my lack of talent, as I don't have any special skills. I worked first with the Carmelite sisters in Washington. I'd do two nights a week at a shelter for women who were mostly drug addicts, alcoholics, ex-prostitutes, and people just out of prison. It was a dangerous place but I learned a lot about the homeless. You know, we tend to see them as visitors from another planet. We never think of hunkering down and talking to them, because we think they might be violent or mentally unbalanced; but from my experience those are usually in the minority. Most of them are quiet, gentle people where something has just gone wrong. They are vulnerable and more endangered than dangerous.

"When Mother Teresa visited Washington a few years back, I remember her on Capitol Hill at this congressional reception when a senator said to her, 'Mother, you're doing marvelous work.' She replied,

'It's God's work.' He then said, 'But in India, where there are so many problems, can you ever be successful at what you do—isn't it hopeless to try?' She replied, 'Well, Senator, we're not always called to be successful but we're always called to be faithful.' Her answer really hit me to the core.

"Then, when we moved to Europe, I approached the Missionaries of Charity sisters, who offered me a job volunteering in London, and this is where I have been ever since. Every morning I am delighted to be here—it's a surprise to me but it is true. I think, Thank God, and let's get started. I'm always happy to start the day, unlike the way I felt at other jobs I had—secular, paying jobs—where I would always be discontented. Here what I am doing is compatible with what I'm thinking inside. There's no conflict between feeling and thinking and doing."

GERRY

"I've found out that to think about changing the world is an impossible and probably arrogant idea. If you don't like it the way it is, then change yourself. That's what I've done within my family and my work and my life. Through changing myself I can touch others more closely. I used to be a chain smoker weighing 210 pounds, and I took myself in hand to stop destroying myself. I took up running and lost weight and became much healthier.

"A few years back, when I was running, a little bug used to be in my ear saying, 'You've got to do something for God.' I had no idea what to do. Then I saw an item in our parish bulletin that said: 'Wanted, young man to help nuns in South Bronx in young men's shelter.' So I gave them a ring and went down there. I said, 'Sister, I'm looking for the shelter,' and she said, 'Go round the corner.' She obviously assumed I needed help. The sisters have a rule that we take in the people from last night first and all new people wait until the very end. So here I am, I'm looking at all these helpless, homeless drug addicts, alcoholics, and I go walking right up front when they open the door and they say, 'Please wait.' So I think, All right, I'll wait—and I get back in my car, because it's a little chilly. People are standing out there and after about three times and them telling me to still wait, I'm getting irked—maybe I'll pack it in. It's cold, getting dark, and I'm thinking, What am I standing here for? I'm the last one.

"Finally, I ring the bell. They open the door and I say, 'My name is Gerry, I've come to volunteer.' They say, 'Oh, we've been waiting for you!' and that's when I knew they had me, because the sister said, 'You've been in the cold with the poor.' And I've been at that door twice a week now for thirteen years. Every time I have to tell a guy to wait, 'Just be patient,' I'm always very conscious of how that feels.

"Now I am a full-time volunteer and have helped open homes for the sisters in other parts of the States, including New Mexico with the Navajo Indians.

When I first began volunteering and dealt with drunken men who came to the door I found it very difficult to see Jesus in the distressing disguise of the poor. But I found that I had to keep trying, keep looking, and keep going because the poor here are not like those in Calcutta and Mexico. Here people suffer more from a spiritual poverty, which can perhaps be attributed to moral decay and the fact that, if you are poor, you just don't fit in. That's why we do what we do in the South Bronx; but we don't get a lot of volunteers because we need them to live here permanently and most don't want to do that in this area."

KATIE AND KEN

"Ken's grandparents were from India and we wanted to visit them. We decided not to go on a normal tourist trip but to spend some time while we were there working with the sisters in Calcutta. Since then we've been volunteering at their home here in London.

"Last year, when we were on holiday in Israel, we thought we'd visit Nablus, in the Israeli-occupied territories, where the sisters are working in very difficult circumstances, looking after children and old people from Palestinian refugee camps. We were advised not to go because it's a dangerous spot, but since we were in the country and it was only about 50 miles north of Jerusalem, there was no way we were going to stay in Jerusalem and not go and visit them.

"We didn't do anything much apart from taking a few things for them, but I think they were very pleased that we took the trouble. They have a nice house in its own grounds with five sisters and an old Italian priest living in it. But they're very much on their own there and have been under threat, even from the Palestinians—who originally thought they were Jewish settlers because their blue-and-white saris look like the Israeli flag! The Palestinians used to stone them but now they bring their handicapped children and their old people out to them.

"We've certainly learned a great deal from helping the sisters with their work. One of these lessons is that you become *less* vulnerable when you concern yourself with other people's vulnerability rather than your own. We've found that when we're fully involved with helping others, all around the place, we haven't really got time to worry about our own fears—and so they fall into perspective."

NIGEL

"I first met Mother in 1969 when our school priest invited her to visit. He had been studying for the priesthood in Rome and had got involved in the work the sisters were doing there. I was thirteen and she looked like any other old lady to me, but I remember that what she said in the chapel after Mass that day seemed different.

"Our priest organized parties from our school to

go to Italy and work alongside the sisters there. At that time, in the early seventies, there were still shanty-towns in Italy. The kids didn't have a lot to do and were on their own in tragic circumstances. We'd orga-nize sports activities and all sorts of things for them—and they had a great time.

"After I left university, I wanted to put something back into society. So I decided to spend some time working with the sisters. It was an extremely rich experience—although I think it took me about two years to begin to fathom what it was all about. I liked the sisters' joy especially, but also the way they got on with people so well.

"We lived in pretty cramped conditions in the house in Kilburn, London, but it attracted many people, not only the homeless, but also young people, old people, all sorts of people who wanted to get in-volved. And at the other end of the neighborhood there was a shelter with 14 beds in it for homeless men. Every so often, the sisters would organize out-ings. We'd go round at five-thirty in the morning, on the highways and byways, distributing invitations. Anybody who wanted to come, came. I liked that.

"When you got to know the characters, I found you looked past the labels we use like 'alcoholic,' or 'drug addict'—you saw the people and they became friends. Nobody was trying to sell them anything. Mother says that in all the houses all over the world they freely give what is freely given. That for me is very beautiful. A lot of the people who came and stayed in the house said, 'Do we have to pay?' or 'Does the government pay for it?' They said, 'How can it be free?' And we said, 'Because it's freely given.'

"I had a lot of family problems at one time. My mother was seriously ill for eight years. Mental illness, depression, and Parkinson's disease. You know, everything thrown at you at once. I found that when I had to bathe my mother it broke down barriers. And, don't ask me to explain, but when my mother was weak, I got quite strong. I went for a holiday back to the home in Kilburn and I found that working in that environment with a lot of people I already knew made me strong enough to go home and look after my own family. When my mother died I went back to the men at the home in Kilburn—all the old boys were there for *me*, and there was much warmth and comfort.

"A lot of people I know who would like to volunteer, do something to help others, usually then don't want the problems that may accompany that step. The sisters have houses in all sorts of places where there is political strife and threats of violence, and some say, 'I don't want to go there—it's unsafe.' But I say go there anyway, get in touch with reality, through the Missionaries of Charity or whatever vehicle you can find. Most of us fear even going out and knocking on our neighbor's door—many of us don't even know our neighbors. Take the risk: some may ask you to go away but some may offer friendship. And through contact a lot of problems that people carry by themselves can be resolved. It's impossible to be lonely if you reach out to someone else, especially in your community. It's a mutual thing—you give and you receive."

MARY

"I had been volunteering at Kalighat and felt such closeness with the people there. It was such a privilege to serve in the home for the dying, to contact the poor in that way, to have crossed the enormous divide between East and West, between cultures, between classes, and to actually touch someone at the level you are able to do there. When I returned from India to London I went into shock—I noticed how things were so much more man-made, sterile, organized. But I tried to carry on contacting the poor here although it was harder. For instance, every day when I walked to work I would pass a homeless man under the viaduct. One day I noticed another person leave a thermos flask and some sandwiches in the morning on his way to the office and then pick up the flask on his way back. So I thought I'd add an orange—I did this every day and just said 'Hello,' and by doing this I felt a spiritual contact was made with the sisters—I don't feel the divide of countries or cultures so much now. As Mother Teresa says, 'We're just pebbles being thrown into the sea and causing ripples,' and one ripple can be made by one small act of service, and that is the start of many, isn't it?"

GERALDINE

Here, one of the volunteers in Los Angeles describes how she helped the brothers on one of their missions—and discovered what at first seemed another world. But like the previous speakers she, too, learned how in helping someone else you may also help yourself.

"One day I offered to help the brothers on their rounds, and experienced a day I will not soon forget.

"Each Saturday and Sunday, the brothers and Missionaries of Charity co-workers distribute food to the homeless on the streets. On the day I went with them to help, Brother Luke was driving the van and, as we pulled into an alley, he said, 'Prepare yourselves, because this place is awful—we call it Hotel Hell.' As we approached the hotel all we could see was mountains of garbage. Initially, we only saw one woman sitting inside a box shelter. Brother Luke and I got out of the van and the stench of garbage and urine was incredible. We walked into this abandoned hotel, and there was an open courtyard that was also full of garbage. We began yelling that we had food and drinks. Slowly the people living there began to come out towards us. They were so needy—their bodies were emaciated, they were ill, hungry, and they lived in this place that seemed like Hell. For me, seeing them come from this building reminded me of a horror movie, as if they were coming back from the dead. I was overcome with the sight, the smell, and the utter despair of it all.

"While I was handing out fruit and sandwiches a

woman called Margarita approached me. She was ill, holding her throat and barely able to speak. She asked if I knew where she could find a clinic to get some medicine, and of course I didn't. I asked Brother Luke to come over and he said we could call a doctor they knew who would do street calls. Margarita told us that she lived on a mattress under a tree on the other side of the hotel. We assured her that we would return with help. After we got into the van the tears began to flow and I couldn't turn them off. I was crying at the despair and hopelessness; it seemed worse than anything I'd seen in years.

"Dr. Bill, a co-worker who was a trauma doc at one of the Los Angeles hospitals, arrived at around nine that evening. We immediately went out to find Margarita. She was lying on her mattress just outside Hotel Hell. By now she was delirious, with a fever of at least 104°. Being on these streets at this time was a whole new experience for me. Just 10 feet away there were drug deals going down and the activity surrounding us seemed almost clandestine. Dr. Bill was explaining Margarita's medication regimen to another homeless woman. While he was doing that, I went to Margarita and found her coiled in a tight fetal position, her entire body shaking. There were filthy blankets around her and flies like you see on the starving in Africa. I knelt down next to her and began stroking her forearm in a gentle loving way. I did so for three or four minutes. To my amazement I sensed that she was relaxing. Her body unfolded and her tremors ceased. She appeared peaceful and calm despite the fact that she was very ill and probably experiencing withdrawal from crack. Being ill, she was not able to prostitute herself to support her drug addiction.

"It has taken me a lot of time to assimilate what occurred. I do believe that we are channels of God's healing energy and that we can pass that on to one another. What I am not so sure of is who was healed in this situation. When I arrived in Los Angeles I felt fragmented because of the chaos of leaving my job of eighteen years and dealing with many levels of grief over a variety of issues. The experience with Margarita was significant in that I had not wept for anyone else's pain for a long time. Wallowing in my own pain, as justified as it may have been for a while, seemed all too insignificant in the light of what I had experienced at Hotel Hell.

"I felt a real connectedness to Margarita. The next day we visited her, took her some chicken soup and clean water to drink. She was slowly improving and so grateful for our help. And I began to ask myself, Why Margarita and not me? My intellect told me there were no easy answers to this mystery of life. I think the challenge for me is to create a life that speaks of living this mystery."

PETER

"When I was twelve I saw a film about Gladys Ailwood, who was a chambermaid with no money or qualifications but was determined to be a missionary.

She eventually went to China, where, during the war, she took more than 200 children over the mountains in order to rescue them from the fighting. And I thought, That's what I want to do one day!

"As most teenagers do I drifted away from the Church and worked in the fashion industry. I was a photographic model during the punk era in the seventies—a strange business to be in but I had a great time.

"One day I just wanted a bit of peace and something told me to go into a church. It was a normal service but towards the end the priest was talking about this lady called Mother Teresa and all these sisters. I had never heard of her and thought I wanted to find out more. So I went to the Missionaries of Charity house in London and met the superior, who said, 'When would you like to start? How about next Saturday?' Now I've been working with the sisters for over thirteen years and they are like my own sisters—I'd do anything for them.

"I think I was looking for something, something where I could be of some use to people. Being with the sisters in the soup kitchen, on the night run, and talking with the people on the street, I just knew what I was doing was right for me.

"My priorities have changed completely. I decided after a while that I wanted to work in a caring profession, even though I knew the money would be literally a quarter of what I had been earning. Now I work at a cancer hospital in London. I'm an orderly, so I mainly take people in and out of the operating theater. I see people who don't complain when they've got a hell of a lot to complain about—they've got such guts. Sometimes I get people coming up to me who may be bereaved, and they confide in me and I don't even know them. It's like counseling, it just comes naturally—I don't think about it until afterwards.

"The people at the hospital know about what I do with the Missionaries of Charity and they are very good and provide a lot of medical supplies to send to Calcutta. I sponsor some children, as many as I can on my salary, and I get a lot of stuff sent to me by Walt Disney—toys and badges for the kids at Shishu Bhavan.

"I think eventually I've come to realize that the fewer possessions you have the happier you are. When you see the simple way the sisters live it can totally change your life. It's the simplicity, that's what I love. I believe the simplest way is the easiest way to God."

I am always happy when I hear stories of others who offer service where they perceive the need. A group of young Hindu men came to me the other day and said that they had decided to form a society called HOPE whose aim was to help the hopeless. So they put all their money together and went to the market and bought 70 mattresses for the prisoners in the jail. They sacrificed their money to give this gift and never told anybody where the gift came from.

The prayers below are favorites of mine. I send

them out to our co-workers, to volunteers, and give
them to people who visit, to guide and help them
as they serve others.

❧

Dear Lord, help me to spread thy fragrance every-
    where I go.
Flood my soul with Thy spirit and life.
Penetrate and possess my whole being so utterly that
    all my life may only be a radiance of Thine.
Shine through me, and be so in me that every soul I
    come in contact with may feel Thy presence in
    my soul.
Let them look up and see no longer me but only Thee
    O Lord!
Stay with me, and then I shall begin to shine as Thou
    shinest; so to shine as to be a light to others.
The light O Lord will be all from Thee; none of it will
    be mine;
It will be Thou, shining on others through me.
Let me thus praise Thee in the way Thou dost love
    best, by shining on those around me.
Let me preach Thee without preaching, not by words
    but by my example, by the catching force,
        the sympathetic influence of what I do, the evi-
        dent fullness of the love my heart bears to Thee.
          JOHN HENRY CARDINAL NEWMAN

❧

Make us worthy, Lord, to serve our fellow men

throughout the world who live and die in poverty and hunger. Give them, through our hands, this day their daily bread; and by our understanding love, give peace and joy.

POPE PAUL VI

PEACE

THE
FRUIT
OF
SERVICE
IS
PEACE

Works of love are always works of peace. Whenever you share love with others, you'll notice the peace that comes to you and to them. When there is peace, there is God—that is how God touches our lives and shows His love for us by pouring peace and joy into our hearts.

> Lead me from death to life,
> From falsehood to truth.
> Lead me from despair to hope,
> From fear to truth.
> Lead me from hate to love,
> From war to peace.
> Let peace fill our hearts,
> Our world our universe
> Peace peace peace.

Many of our homes around the world are called either "Gift of Love" or "Gift of Peace" because of the gratitude we feel towards God for His grace. We offer these homes as places of comfort for the poor, but it is only God who can complete our work, as Sister Dolores and then Brother Geoff explain:

"Both physical and spiritual healing must be provided for anyone who comes to Nirmal Hriday. We can give touch and comfort and strength in physical healing, but for spiritual healing we need to turn to God. So, knowing our strengths and our weaknesses, we turn to the Lord because all of us carry our past hurts, and He has the remedy for everything. It's simple: If we just turn to Him, He will bring us this inner healing, this spiritual healing so we can make our lives more holy and more pleasing to God."

"If we aim to help a sick person physically, and all our care is devoted to him, is properly motivated by our efforts to love him, then it has a spiritual effect as well. With physical healing one sees the disease and determines how much medicine is needed. These are logical and rational steps. On the spiritual side, as there is no judgment, you let happen whatever is going to happen spiritually, and the more loving you are towards that person the more something will happen spiritually to them and to you. It is always better to expect nothing. Let God work in His own way and then things do happen. Certainly I have seen people expressing this change, showing that in some way they are more aware of God's love for them. It mightn't be in words but is evident in their behavior: a peace descends upon them. For instance many handicapped people are quite self-destructive—beating their heads on the wall and tearing their clothes and mattresses—but when they are given a little more attention or treated more gently, then a notable change occurs. We never really know what is going on inside them but we are aware that some healing is taking place deep within them."

This spiritual healing seems to affect so many people with whom we work—the healers and the healed share God's peace. Sarah, one of the volunteers in our AIDS homes in the United States, shares some observations from her work with us and how it has affected her:

"The people who come into this house, knowing that the end result is that they're dying, find a very peaceful place in which to rest—where if they have even an inkling of a desire to know God, they can get to know Him in any way that suits them. For instance, some believe in reincarnation, some don't. We have long conversations together about God and the afterlife, compare ideas about this life and what we could imagine the next to be. Everyone I've talked to believes in God very much. Sometimes, especially when they are close to death, they embrace the sisters' faith and ask to be baptized, but it is never forced upon them.

"I've found that working here puts the things in my life in perspective, in balance. When I'm in the office I'm in the so-called real world, but then when I started volunteering with the Missionaries of Charity one day a week, I realized that this was the real world, not the other. The home isn't a glamorous or beautiful place but the people here are real live human beings who are being born again because they're dying. The people downtown are alive but they're not really living at all.

"Working in the home has made me learn what is important in this life and realize there is a life after this one. A lot of people I know go through life not even giving the afterlife a flicker of a thought. One thing that God has shown me is that He loves everybody, so who am I to judge another? My life, as a result of volunteering with the Missionaries of Charity sisters, is deeper, richer, and much more balanced between the material and the spiritual. I've found peace."

Sister Dolores adds her experiences of God's peace from working with the dying:

"A lot of men who come to our AIDS homes arrive full of despair. But after the tender care of our sisters and the volunteers they find peace in their hearts. So it is really a homecoming for them when they come to our houses. Many say, 'This will be the last place I'll live, the last place I'll be,' and I have always said, 'No, this is the last but one. From here you have to go to your true home where our heavenly Father is waiting.' And many long to go.

"When I'm with a person in his last moments and everything is peaceful as he leaves this world, I'm reminded that we all have to go through this at some point. I have a great longing to be able to go peacefully, in this beautiful way, myself. We are all meant to return to God—we come from Him and we go back to Him—so by assisting others in their final moments, we ourselves are being helped."

Sister Theresina remembers a man who visited the home in London and wrote her a letter:

"After he had been to see us he wrote saying that he had found with us what he couldn't buy or even find himself—spiritual peace. He said that he'd experienced a lot of wealth in his life and at those times he'd had the least amount of peace."

BY
FORGETTING
YOURSELF
YOU
FIND
YOURSELF

We have a right to be happy and peaceful. We have been created for this—we are born to be happy—and we can only find true happiness and peace when we are in love with God: there is joy in loving God, great happiness in loving Him. Many people think, especially in the West, that having money makes you happy. I think it must be harder to be happy if you are wealthy because you may find it difficult to see God: you'll have too many other things to think about. However, if God has given you this gift of wealth, then use it for His purpose—help others, help the poor, create jobs, give work to others. Don't waste your wealth. Having food, a home, dignity, freedom, health, and an education are all of God's gifts too, which is why we must help those who are less fortunate than ourselves.

Jesus said, "What you did to the least of my brethren, you did it to me." Therefore, the only sadness I ever feel is if I do something wrong, if I hurt Our Lord in some way, through selfishness or uncharitableness, for instance. When we hurt the poor, and we hurt each other, we're hurting God.

Everything is God's to give and to take away, so share what you've been given, and that includes yourself. The following poem was written by one of our resident AIDS patients in San Francisco and is about the joy of sharing and of friendship:

Being a friend, I do not care, not I,
How gods or men wrong me, beat me down.
His words are a sufficient star to travel by.
I count him with quiet praise.
Being a friend, I do not covet gold,
Or the royal gift to give him pleasure, but
Sit with him and have him hold my hand.
Is wealth, I think, passing the mint, treasure?
Being a friend, I only covet art,
A white pure flame to search me as I trace,
In crooked letters from a throbbing heart,
The hymn to beauty written on his face.
Though a seeker since my birth,
Here is all I've learned on Earth
It's the gift of what I know—
Give advice to buy a foe.
Random truths are all I find,
Stuck like burrs about my mind—

Solve a blister, burn an old letter.
And the youth said "Speak to us of friendship"
And he answered saying,
"Your friend is your needs answered.
He's your field which you sow with love
And reap with thanksgiving.
And he is your board and your fireside,
For you to come to with your hunger,
Seeking him for peace."

Be happy in the moment, that's enough. Each moment
is all we need, not more. Be happy now and if you
show through your actions that you love others, including those who are poorer than you, you'll give
them happiness, too. It doesn't take much—it can be
just giving a smile. The world would be a much better
place if everyone smiled more. So smile, be cheerful,
be joyous that God loves you.

The following is the prayer of peace written by
St. Francis of Assisi, which we say each day. It is a re-
minder of how we can create peace in our lives by giving ourselves, with an open and clean heart, to others:

Lord, make me a channel of Thy peace, that
Where there is hatred, I may bring love;
That where there is wrong, I may bring the spirit of
    forgiveness;
That where there is discord, I may bring harmony;
That where there is error, I may bring truth;
That where there is doubt, I may bring faith;

That where there is despair, I may bring hope;
That where there are shadows, I may bring light;
That where there is sadness, I may bring joy.
Lord, grant that I may seek rather to comfort than to
    be comforted,
To understand than to be understood;
To love than to be loved.
For it is by forgetting self that one finds;
It is by forgiving that one is forgiven;
It is by dying that one awakens to eternal life.

Here are some closing words from our volunteers Dave, John, and Rupert, who have found joy and peace by help- ing the poor:

"Since I began working here in London I get so much more than I give. There's a joy in my work, but it's not a barrel of laughs or a party—joy has a serious side to it. It can be lighthearted and casual and also a deep-seated peaceful joy like the kind a father and mother would experience at the birth of their child, or what you feel on the day you get married. I'm happy and joyful to be here but I take it seriously—the work is serious—though I'm not anxious about it. I'm a much calmer and more relaxed person now that I'm doing work for others."

"Working in Kalighat was a life-changing experi- ence for me. I thought I was going to go for a day but after I'd done that I decided I wanted to go every day for a month. I just knew that every afternoon when I was finished and relaxing, I felt as though I was in Heaven. I'm not saying that's how the sisters feel, doing it every day, but I just experienced another aspect of life that was available to me. The work gives a certain sense which is somehow beyond an ordinary feeling—I don't know how to describe it really, it was just peace. Tremendous peace would descend upon me every single day."

"I have become a full human being since having the opportunity of working with the Missionaries of Charity. Nobody is better than another—it's just that I learned to respond with humanity to each situation and its limitations. The more you give the more you get. And all the time you're giving, loving, and helping, more is given to the world, more than we'd ever know from our one small step. It's like having a kind of empathy with the heart of the world."

Finally, I have only one message of peace and that is to love one another as God loves each one of you. Jesus came to give us the good news that God loves us and that He wants us to love one another. And when the time comes to die and go home to God again, we will hear Him say, "Come and possess the Kingdom prepared for you, because I was hungry and you gave me to eat, I was naked and you clothed me, I was sick and you visited me. Whatever you did to the least of my brethren, you did it to me."

GOD BLESS YOU
Mother Teresa

ANYWAY

People are unreasonable, illogical, and self-centered,
LOVE THEM ANYWAY
If you do good, people will accuse you of
selfish, ulterior motives,
DO GOOD ANYWAY
If you are successful,
you win false friends and true enemies,
SUCCEED ANYWAY
The good you do will be forgotten tomorrow,
DO GOOD ANYWAY
Honesty and frankness make you vulnerable,
BE HONEST AND FRANK ANYWAY
What you spent years building may be
destroyed overnight,
BUILD ANYWAY
People really need help
but may attack you if you help them,
HELP PEOPLE ANYWAY
Give the world the best you have
and you'll get kicked in the teeth,
GIVE THE WORLD THE BEST YOU'VE GOT ANYWAY.

From a sign on the wall of Shishu Bhavan, the children's home in
Calcutta

APPENDICES

APPENDIX
I

IMPORTANT
DATES

1910   Mother Teresa born Agnes Gonxha
            Bojaxhiu in Skopje, Albania, on Au-
            gust 26.

1928   Entered the Sisters of Loreto order in
            Ireland and began her novitiate in Dar-
            jeeling, India.

1929–1948   Geography teacher at St. Mary's High
            School in Calcutta and for some years
            principal of the school.

1948   Received permission from the Catholic
            Church to live outside the school and
            serve the "poorest of the poor" in the
            streets of Calcutta.

1949	Took Indian citizenship.
1950	The congregation of the Missionaries of Charity (sisters) was approved by the Catholic Church and instituted in Calcutta.
1952	Founded the first home in India, Nirmal Hriday, on the Feast of the Immaculate Heart of Mary.
1953	Moved to the Mother House in Lower Circular Road, Calcutta.
1960	By this year, twenty-five homes had been opened in India.
1965	The Missionaries of Charity became a Society of Pontifical Right in Rome.
	The first home outside India opened in Cocorote, Venezuela.
1966	The Missionaries of Charity Brothers was founded under Brother Andrew, the first General Servant.
1968	Homes opened in Rome and Tanzania.

1969	Founded the International Association of Co-Workers, opened homes in Australia, and started extensive overseas expansion.
1971	First home opened in the United States in the South Bronx, New York.
	Awarded the Pope John XXIII Peace Prize.
1975	The Brothers opened their first home outside Calcutta in Vietnam.
1976	Founded the Contemplative branch of the Missionaries of Charity, called "Sisters of the Word."
1977	The Brothers opened a home in Hong Kong and started others in Asia.
1979	Awarded the Nobel Peace Prize.
1980	From this year homes were opened for drug addicts, prostitutes, and battered women around the world.
	Campaigned against abortion by promoting adoption.

Built orphanages and schools for poor children.

1985   Established a hospice for people with AIDS in New York.

1986   Founded the Lay Missionaries of Charity branch.

1988   Sent Missionaries of Charity to work in Russia.

Opened a home for people with AIDS in San Francisco.

1991   Mother Teresa returned for the first time to her native Albania (Serbia) and opened a home in Tirana.

By this year there were 168 homes established in India.

1995   Expansion continued with plans progressing to open in China.

APPENDIX
II

THE
MISSIONARIES
OF
CHARITY
ORDER

The order is composed of eight branches:
    the Active Sisters
    the Contemplative Sisters
    the Active Brothers
    the Contemplative Brothers
    the Missionary Fathers
    the Lay Missionaries
    the Volunteers and the Sick and Suffering Co-
        Workers

The Active and Contemplative Sisters are required to train for up to six years. This training is as follows:

ASPIRANCY   Six months.

POSTULANCY   Up to a year.

NOVITIATE   Two years. First vows are taken after this novitiate, which makes a woman a Professed Sister.

JUNIORATE   Five years. Vows are renewed each year.

TERTIANSHIP   The sixth year of vows, after which the final vows are taken. Before final vows, the sister goes home for three weeks to give her the opportunity to decide if she wishes to remain and serve as a Missionary of Charity for life.

The novitiate training takes place in Calcutta, Rome, Manila, Nairobi, San Francisco, and Poland.

The Active Sisters spend their day in service to the poorest of the poor. The Contemplative Sisters pray most of the day except for two hours when they also do service in the community. The sisters report to their regional superiors and sometimes directly to Mother Teresa.

❧

The Missionaries of Charity Brothers and Fathers are separate congregations from the sisters but share the same spirit and vow of wholehearted free service to the poorest of the poor. The Brothers report to the General Servant (the head of their order) or to their regional superiors. The Fathers report to their Superior General.

The Missionaries of Charity Brothers have a two-year novitiate after the initial "come and see" period, which lasts from three to twelve months. There is no obligatory postulant period for the brothers. The brothers are the more active, doing similar work to that of the sisters.

The Fathers are more contemplative, praying and saying Mass. They are either already ordained priests or those training to be priests with the Missionaries of Charity. They have a two-year novitiate before repeating their vows to a new congregation, if they are priests before joining the order.

❧

The Lay Missionaries of Charity make their lives in the world but take the same vows over the same length of time as the sisters. They can be associated with the apostolate work of the Missionaries of Charity directly, or they can find their own Apostolate to live out their fourth vow to give "wholehearted free service to the poorest of the poor" for their lives. They are religious people but can be either single or married with families.

❧

The Co-Workers are volunteers with deep spiritual commitment who share the vision of the work of the Missionaries of Charity and wish to live "radiating God's love" in voluntary poverty and in sacrifice of luxuries. They work alongside members of the order, reporting to the Regional Superior. They live their lives in prayer and service to their families as well as the community. Priests, too, can volunteer as co-workers—they have been referred to as "the spiritual heart of the co-workers as a family." Pope John Paul II asked to be the first priest to be accepted into the priest adoption program, whereby a priest and sister adopt each other in prayer. Anyone of any religious denomination can join the co-workers.

The Sick and Suffering Co-Workers are members of an association formed in 1969 through a woman called Jacqueline de Decker who, because of sickness and disability, was unable to join in the active work of the co-workers. Instead, the Sick and Suffering Co-Workers offer their sufferings for the poor and for the work of the Missionaries of Charity among them. Their prayers provide spiritual sustenance to the active missionaries in carrying out their work. They become "second selves" to the missionaries, those who pray for the work of the other.

The official language of all the Missionaries of Charity is English.

ACKNOWLEDGMENTS

I greatly appreciate the time, taken away from their real work of helping the poor, that Mother Teresa and the sisters and brothers of the Missionaries of Charity gave in talking to us. I am very grateful to the volunteers from many parts of the world, some of whom we were fortunate enough to work alongside, who shared their experiences with us. In India we received help and advice from Naresh and Sunita Kumar, Michael and Jane Anthony, and members of Omer Ahmed's family. My thanks to Random House for their encouragement and support, especially Fiona MacIntyre and Judith Kendra. A special thank-you to Nix Picasso for her ideas, her help with interviews, and her dedication; to Emma Lever for her research and transcription of interviews, and to my wife, Pene, for her help and advice in all areas. I much enjoyed collaborating with

Lucinda Vardey, and also acknowledge Omer Ahmed, Tony Allen, Gerald and Jane Bray, Enid Davidge, Jean Maclean, Bob and Neil Maclean, and Richard Taylor, who each know the contribution they have made. Finally, I thank my parents for their support and encouragement and my young daughters for waiting patiently to spend time with their father.

JOHN CAIRNS

I wish to thank the following people who have helped me with this project: my friend and agent, Carolyn Brunton, for suggesting me as writer for this book; Judith Kendra of Rider Books, Random House, for having confidence in me and for introducing me so well to the amorphism of Calcutta life; Ann Petrie for her generosity, support, and wise counsel; Sister Priscilla for her encouragement and cooperation and John Cairns for his conviction, commitment, and tireless traveling to gain the contents for this book. My husband, John Dalla Costa, has advised me, supported me, and guided me to a deeper understanding of Christian life. Finally, my eternal gratitude to Mother Teresa herself for her generosity of spirit and time, and for sharing her faith.

LUCINDA VARDEY